UK Slow Cooker Cookbook with Pictures

1200 Days Super Easy, Tasty and Affordable Homemade Slow Cooker Recipes for Beginners Eat Healthy Every Day (Colour Edition)

Richard Green

ISBN: 979-8325127304

TABLE OF CONTENT

INTRODUCTION

Hey there, I'm Richard Green, a dedicated home cook and a proud dad of two. Cooking has always been a labor of love for me, and there's nothing I enjoy more than preparing delicious, wholesome meals for my family. As a parent, I know that finding the balance between a hectic schedule and serving mouthwatering dishes can be a daily challenge.

This cookbook, is my way of sharing the secrets and joys of slow cooking with you. Whether you're a seasoned chef or just starting on your culinary journey, slow cooking can revolutionise the way you approach family meals.

Why slow cooking? Well, the answer is simple: it's a lifesaver for busy families like ours. The slow cooker, with its set-and-forget approach, has been my trusty sidekick for years. It's a culinary magician that transforms simple ingredients into rich, flavourful dishes, all while allowing you to focus on other aspects of your life.

In this cookbook, I'll guide you through the wonderful world of slow cooking, sharing tips, techniques, and, of course, a delightful collection of recipes that my own family has enjoyed over the years. From comforting breakfasts to hearty dinners and irresistible desserts, there's something for every meal and occasion.

I'll introduce you to various types of slow cookers, provide essential tips for getting the most out of your appliance, and explore the diverse recipes that can simplify your daily meal prep. Whether it's a cozy family dinner, a weekend brunch, or a special holiday feast, the slow cooker has a role to play.

So, join me on this culinary journey as we unlock the potential of your slow cooker and rediscover the joy of cooking wholesome, flavourful meals that bring families closer. Let's savour the moments, flavours, and simplicity that slow cooking can offer, all while making the most of our precious time together. Thank you for letting me be a part of your culinary adventure.

CHAPTER 1
GETTING TO KNOW YOUR SLOW COOKER

The Different Types of Slow Cookers

When it comes to choosing the right slow cooker for your kitchen, you'll find a variety of options to consider. The type of slow cooker that suits your needs largely depends on your cooking style, the size of your family, and your budget. Here, we'll explore the most common types:

- **Basic Manual Slow Cooker: This is the classic slow cooker that features manual controls. It typically has three temperature settings:** low, high, and warm. It's a straightforward choice for those who prefer simplicity and don't require fancy features.

- **Programmable Slow Cooker:** Programmable slow cookers offer more control over the cooking process. They allow you to set a specific cook time, after which the cooker switches to a "warm" mode to keep your meal hot until you're ready to serve. These are great for busy families with varying schedules.

- **Multi-Cooker (Slow Cooker/Pressure Cooker Combo):** A multi-cooker is a versatile kitchen appliance that combines slow cooking with pressure cooking and often includes other functions like sautéing and steaming. It's perfect for those who want a single device that can do it all.

- **Connectivity and Smart Slow Cookers:** In this digital age, you can find slow cookers that can be controlled remotely through smartphone apps. These high-tech devices offer convenience and precision, allowing you to adjust cooking settings from anywhere.

- **Portable Slow Cooker:** These are designed for on-the-go cooking. They typically have a secure lid and locking mechanism to prevent spills during transport. They're great for potlucks, picnics, or taking your meal to a gathering.

Features and Functions of Slow Cooker

No matter which type of slow cooker you choose, they all share common features and functions that make slow cooking a breeze. Here's a breakdown of the key components:

- **Cooking Pot/Insert:** The heart of your slow cooker, the cooking pot (often ceramic or metal) is where your ingredients go. It's removable for easy cleaning and may have a non-stick coating.

- **Heating Element:** This is located under the cooking pot and is responsible for heating the contents. The insulation around the heating element helps maintain a consistent temperature.

- **Lid:** The lid keeps heat and moisture trapped inside, which is crucial for slow cooking. Most lids are made of transparent glass, allowing you to check on your meal without lifting it.

- **Temperature Settings:** Slow cookers usually offer at least two temperature settings: "low" for gentle, all-day cooking and "high" for faster cooking. Some models also have a "warm" setting to keep food hot without overcooking it.

- **Timer:** Programmable slow cookers feature timers, allowing you to set a specific cooking duration. When the timer runs out, the slow cooker automatically switches to the "warm" setting.

- **Stoneware vs. Metal:** Slow cookers come with either stoneware or metal cooking pots. Stoneware pots are excellent for even heating and retaining flavours, while metal pots heat up more quickly and may be more durable.

Understanding the different types and features of slow cookers is the first step to maximizing your slow cooking experience. With the right device in your kitchen, you'll be well-equipped to prepare delicious, stress-free meals for your family. In the following chapters, we'll dive into the practical aspects of using your slow cooker and explore a wide range of recipes that showcase its versatility.

How to Choose the Perfect Slow Cooker

Choosing the perfect slow cooker is a crucial step in harnessing the power of this versatile appliance. With various types and features available, here are some tips to help you select the ideal slow cooker for your specific needs:

- **Consider Size and Capacity:** Think about the number of people you typically cook for. Slow cookers come in various sizes, usually measured in litres. A 3.5 to 5.5-litre slow cooker is ideal for most families, but you can go smaller for couples or larger for big gatherings.

- **Type of Cooking:** Determine what you'll use the slow cooker for most. If you plan on using it mainly for one-pot meals, a simple manual slow cooker will suffice. However, if you want versatility, a multi-cooker might be a better choice.

- **Programmability:** If you're away from home for extended periods, consider a programmable slow cooker. These allow you to set cooking times and switch to "warm" automatically, preventing overcooking.

- **Temperature Settings:** Pay attention to the temperature settings. Most slow cookers have low and high settings, but some models offer additional options. If you want more control, look for a cooker with variable temperature settings.

Advantages of Slow Cooking

Slow cooking is more than just a convenient way to prepare meals; it offers a multitude of advantages, making it the perfect cooking method for busy families. Here's why you should embrace the slow cooker in your kitchen:

- **Time Efficiency:** Slow cooking allows you to save time during meal preparation. You can set your ingredients in the morning, head to work or take care of other responsibilities, and return home to a hot, ready-to-eat meal. This is a game-changer for families with packed schedules.

- **Ease of Use:** Slow cookers are incredibly user-friendly. Just add your ingredients, set the temperature and cooking time, and let the appliance do the work. It's a no-fuss approach that even kids can participate in.

- **Nutrient Retention:** The low and slow cooking method preserves more nutrients in your food compared to rapid high-heat cooking. This ensures that your family enjoys healthier and more flavourful meals.

- **Tender, Flavourful Dishes:** Slow cooking breaks down tough meat fibres and infuses flavours, resulting in succulent, tender dishes. It's an ideal way to transform inexpensive cuts of meat into culinary delights.

Incorporating slow cooking into your family's routine is a wise choice that offers numerous benefits, from delicious and nutritious meals to time-saving convenience. It allows you to savour meals without the hassle, making it the ideal companion for modern families looking to balance their busy lives with home-cooked, wholesome cuisine.

Time and Temperature Settings for Different Dishes

One of the key elements to master in slow cooking is understanding the appropriate time and temperature settings for various dishes. With a bit of guidance, you can create a wide range of family-friendly meals in your slow cooker. Here's a breakdown of the ideal settings for different types of dishes:

1. Soups and Stews:

Temperature: Low
Cooking Time: 6-8 hours
Soups and stews benefit from long, slow cooking, allowing flavours to meld and ingredients to become tender. Start these in the morning, and they'll be ready by dinnertime.

2. Tough Cuts of Meat (Pot Roasts, Brisket, Ribs):

Temperature: Low or High (based on available time)
Cooking Time: Low - 8-10 hours; High - 4-6 hours
Low and slow works best for incredibly tender results. However, if you're short on time, high heat is an acceptable option.

3. Chicken Dishes:

Temperature: Low or High (based on available time)
Cooking Time: Low - 6-8 hours; High - 3-4 hours
Chicken can be slow-cooked on either setting, but be mindful not to overcook to prevent dryness.

4. Vegetarian Dishes (Chilli, Curries, Ratatouille):

Temperature: Low
Cooking Time: 6-8 hours
Slow cooking allows vegetables and spices to meld and create rich, flavourful vegetarian dishes.

5. Pasta Dishes:

Temperature: Low
Cooking Time: 1-2 hours
Pasta should be added in the last hour or so of cooking to prevent overcooking and becoming mushy.

6. Desserts (Cobblers, Puddings, Custards):

Temperature: Low
Cooking Time: 2-3 hours
Low and slow ensures even cooking and prevents burning. Ideal for creating delectable, spoonable desserts.

7. Breakfast Dishes (Porridge, Casseroles, Frittatas):

Temperature: Low
Cooking Time: 6-8 hours (overnight)
Start these dishes the night before for a warm, ready-to-eat breakfast the next morning.

8. Seafood Dishes:

Temperature: Low
Cooking Time: 1-2 hours
Seafood cooks quickly, and slow cooking can easily lead to overdone dishes, so use the low setting for a shorter duration.

9. Side Dishes (Rice, Potatoes, Vegetables):

Temperature: Low
Cooking Time: 2-4 hours
Slow cooking side dishes is a great way to free up hob space while ensuring even cooking.

Remember that these settings are general guidelines. You may need to adjust cooking times based on the specific model of your slow cooker, the size of your ingredients, and your personal preferences. Always check for doneness before serving, and don't be afraid to experiment to find the perfect settings for your favourite family recipes.

CHAPTER 2
BREAKFAST

Western Omelette Bake

Prep time: 15 minutes
Cook time: 8 to 9 hours

INGREDIENTS:
900 g frozen hash brown potatoes
12 eggs
180 g shredded Cheddar cheese
450 g cooked ham, cubed
1 medium onion, diced
235 ml milk
1 tsp. salt
1 tsp. pepper

DIRECTIONS:
1. Layer one-third each of frozen potatoes, ham, onion, and cheese in the bottom of the slow cooker. Repeat 2 times.
2. Beat together eggs, milk, salt, and pepper in a bowl.
3. Pour over mixture in a slow cooker. Cover and cook on low for 8 to 9 hours.
4. Serve with orange juice and fresh fruit, if desired.

Cheesy Baked Eggs

Serve: 6

Prep time: 10 minutes
Cook time: 4 to 6 hours

INGREDIENTS:
6 eggs, beaten
700 ml milk
100 g toasted bread cubes
180 g shredded cheese
Fried, crumbled streaky bacon or ham chunks (optional)
¾ tsp. salt
¼ tsp. pepper

DIRECTIONS:
1. Combine bread cubes, cheese, and meat (if desired) in a greased slow cooker.
2. Mix together eggs, milk, salt, and pepper in a bowl. Pour over bread and cook on low for 4 to 6 hours.
3. Let cool for 5 minutes before serving.

Basic Porridge

Prep time: 5 minutes
Cook time: 6 hours

INGREDIENTS:
10o g dry old-fashioned rolled oats
600 ml water
Dash of salt

DIRECTIONS:
1. Mix together oats, water, and salt in a slow cooker. Cook on low for 6 hours.
2. Stir and serve.

Cheesy Bacon and Egg Hash

Serve: 8 to 10

Prep time: 10 minutes
Cook time: 3 to 4 hours

INGREDIENTS:
Rapeseed oil spray
8 slices thick-cut streaky bacon
30 ml olive oil (if necessary)
230 g sliced white or chestnut mushrooms
12 large eggs or 2 large eggs plus 14 large egg whites
680 to 850 g frozen plain shredded hash brown potatoes, partially thawed
230 g shredded Cheddar cheese
235 ml single cream
80 g soured cream
60 g grated or shredded Parmesan cheese
115 g shredded or sliced Mozzarella cheese
1 bunch spring onions (white part and some of the green), thinly sliced
45 g Dijon mustard
¼ tsp. sea salt
10 grinds freshly ground black or white pepper
Hot sauce, for serving

DIRECTIONS:
1. Cook the bacon in a large frying pan over medium heat until crisp, about 4 minutes. Remove from the frying pan and drain on kitchen towels. Pour off all but 2 tbsps. of the bacon fat. (Or, if not using bacon, add the olive oil to the frying pan.) Add the mushrooms to the frying pan and cook until soft, about 4 minutes.
2. Coat the slow cooker with rapeseed oil spray. Using your fingers, layer the hash browns in the bottom and about 2.5 cm up the sides of the slow cooker. Crumble the bacon and sprinkle it over the hash browns (or overlap prosciutto slices), then add the mushrooms, the cheeses, and half of the spring onions (reserve the rest of the spring onion for garnish).
3. In a medium-size bowl, whisk together the eggs, single cream, soured cream, mustard, salt, and pepper and slowly pour the mixture into the slow cooker. Cover and cook on high for 3 to 4 hours, until the eggs are set and a bit brown around the edges. Sprinkle the remaining spring onions over the top and remove portions with a non-stick spatula. Serve immediately, with or without hot sauce.

Date and Almond Porridge

Prep time: 5 minutes
Cook time: 4 to 6 hours

INGREDIENTS:
950 ml water
160 g dry rolled oats
60 g dry Grape-Nuts cereal
55 g slivered almonds
45 g chopped dates

DIRECTIONS:
1. Combine all the ingredients in a slow cooker. Cook on low for 4 to 6 hours.
2. Serve with fat-free milk, if desired.

Boston Brown Bread

Prep time: 5 minutes
Cook time: 3 to 4 hours

INGREDIENTS:
400 ml buttermilk
160 g black treacle
45 g butter, melted
120 g sultanas
135 g fine white cornmeal
90 g fine wholemeal flour
80 g rye flour
475 ml boiling water
1¾ tsps. bread soda
½ tsp. baking powder
1 tsp. salt
Rapeseed oil spray

DIRECTIONS:
1. Fold four 30 by 20-cm pieces of aluminium foil in half twice to yield rectangles that measure 15 by 10 cm and grease one side with rapeseed oil spray. Coat inside of four 425-g tins with oil spray.
2. Whisk rye flour, fine wholemeal flour, cornmeal, bread soda, baking powder, and salt together in a large bowl. Whisk buttermilk, black treacle, and melted butter together in a second bowl. Stir sultanas into buttermilk mixture. Add buttermilk mixture to flour mixture and stir until combined and no dry flour remains. Divide batter evenly among prepared tins and smooth top with back of greased spoon. Wrap tops of tins tightly with prepared foil, greased side facing batter.
3. Line bottom of a slow cooker with greaseproof paper. Fill the slow cooker with 1¼-cm boiling water (about 475 ml water) and set tins in the slow cooker. Cover and cook until skewer inserted in the centre of loaves comes out clean, 3 to 4 hours on high.
4. Using tongs and sturdy spatula, transfer tins to a wire rack and let cool, uncovered, for 20 minutes. Invert tins and slide loaves onto the rack and let cool completely, about 1 hour. Slice and serve. (Bread can be wrapped tightly in cling film and stored at room temperature for up to 3 days.)

Breakfast Sausage Hash Brown

Prep time: 15 minutes

Cook time: 3 hours

INGREDIENTS:

450 g sweet Italian sausage, casings removed
3 sweet peppers, thinly sliced
900 g rooster potatoes, peeled and grated
120 g grated cheddar cheese
175 ml low-sodium chicken broth
30 g unsalted butter

30 g plain flour
115 ml milk
Coarse salt and freshly ground pepper, to taste
6 spring onions, finely chopped
Fried eggs, for serving
Chopped fresh chives, for garnish

DIRECTIONS:

1. Melt butter in a saucepan over medium heat. Whisk in flour and cook for about 1 minute. Add broth and milk and bring to a boil, whisking constantly. Remove from heat and season with salt and pepper. Transfer sauce to a bowl.
2. Heat the saucepan over medium-high heat. Add sausage and cook, breaking up meat with a spoon, until browned, about 5 minutes. Add peppers and continue to cook until peppers are soft, about 5 minutes. Season with salt and pepper. Transfer to a slow cooker, spreading into an even layer.
3. Add potatoes, cheese, and spring onions to milk mixture and mix well. Transfer to slow cooker and spread into an even layer. Cover and cook on high until hot and bubbly, about 3 hours (or on low for 6 hours). Serve warm, with fried eggs and topped with chives.

Traditional Irish-Style Porridge

Prep time: 5 minutes

Cook time: 3 to 4 hours

INGREDIENTS:

30 g unsalted butter
320 g coarse oatmeal

1.8 L water
1 tsp. salt

DIRECTIONS:

1. Melt butter in a frying pan over medium heat. Add the oatmeal and toast, stirring constantly, until golden and fragrant, about 2 minutes. Transfer to a slow cooker.
2. Stir water and salt into a slow cooker. Cover and cook until the porridge is softened and thickened, 3 to 4 hours on high. Stir the porridge to recombine. Turn off slow cooker and let porridge sit for 10 minutes. Serve. (Porridge can be refrigerated for up to 4 days. Reheat porridge in microwave or in saucepan over medium-low heat; stir often and adjust consistency with hot water as needed.)

Ricotta and Spinach Egg Bake

Prep time: 15 minutes

Cook time: 2 to 3 hours

INGREDIENTS:

1 onion, finely chopped
15 ml extra-virgin olive oil
3 garlic cloves, minced
285 g whole-milk ricotta cheese
230 g frozen chopped spinach, thawed and squeezed dry

115 g Fontina cheese, shredded
4 large eggs, lightly beaten
¼ tsp. salt
¼ tsp. pepper
2 plum tomatoes, cored and sliced crosswise ½-cm thick

DIRECTIONS:

1. Microwave onion, oil, and garlic in a large bowl, stirring occasionally, until onion is softened, about 5 minutes. Stir in ricotta, spinach, Fontina, eggs, salt, and pepper until well combined. Divide mixture evenly among four greased ramekins and scatter tomatoes over top.
2. Fill a slow cooker with 1¼-cm boiling water (about 475 ml water) and set ramekins in the slow cooker. Cover and cook until the eggs are set, 2 to 3 hours on low. Using tongs and sturdy spatula, remove ramekins from slow cooker and let cool for 15 minutes before serving.

Ginger Fish Congee

Prep time: 10 minutes

Cook time: 4⅓ hours

INGREDIENTS:

300 g long-grain white rice
350 g firm white fish fillets, such as flounder or cod, skin removed, thinly sliced
1 (2½-cm) piece fresh ginger,

peeled and grated
3 L boiling water
Coarse salt, to taste
Sliced spring onions, for serving

DIRECTIONS:

1. Place the rice and ginger into the slow cooker. Add the boiling water and stir. Cover and cook on low until congee reaches consistency of loose porridge, about 4 hours (or on high for 2 hours).
2. Add fish and cook on low until fish falls apart, about 20 minutes more (or on high for 10 minutes). Season to taste with salt and serve with the sliced spring onions.

Honey Mango Yoghurt

Serve: 4

Prep time: 5 minutes

Cook time: 2 hours

INGREDIENTS:

1 L milk
2 mangoes, cut into chunks
60 g plain yoghurt

20 g honey
¼ tsp. ground cardamom

DIRECTIONS:

1. Pour the milk into the slow cooker. Cover and cook on low for 2 hours.
2. Turn off the slow cooker and stir in the yoghurt. Cover with the lid and wrap the outside of the slow cooker housing with a bath towel to help insulate it. Allow it to rest for 8 hours or overnight.
3. For a thick yoghurt, strain the mixture in a medium bowl through a few layers of cheesecloth for 10 to 15 minutes. Discard the whey remaining in the cheesecloth or save it for making smoothies.
4. To serve, stir in the mango chunks, honey, and cardamom.

Creamy Cheese Polenta

Serve: 6

Prep time: 5 minutes

Cook time: 2 to 3 hours

INGREDIENTS:

Rapeseed oil spray
700 ml water, plus extra as needed
235 ml whole milk
180 g cornmeal
230 g sharp cheddar cheese,

shredded
120 g butter, softened
4 spring onions, thinly sliced
½ tsp. hot sauce
Salt and pepper, to taste

DIRECTIONS:

1. Lightly coat slow cooker with rapeseed oil spray. Whisk water, milk, cornmeal, and 1 tsp. of salt together in prepared slow cooker. Cover and cook until cornmeal is tender, 2 to 3 hours on high.
2. Whisk cheddar, butter, spring onions, and hot sauce into cornmeal until combined. Season with salt and pepper to taste. Serve. (Polenta can be held on warm or low setting for up to 2 hours; adjust consistency with hot water as needed before serving.)

CHAPTER 3
BEANS AND RICE

Chickpea Curry

Prep time: 10 minutes
Cook time: 10 hours

INGREDIENTS:

15 ml rapeseed oil
350 g dried chickpeas
2 medium tomatoes, finely chopped
2 tsps. cumin seeds
2 bay leaves
7 cm piece cassia bark or cinnamon
2 medium onions, thinly sliced
1 tsp. salt
1 tbsp. freshly grated ginger
950 ml hot water
6 garlic cloves, finely chopped
2 fresh green chillis, chopped

1 tsp. Kashmiri chilli powder
2 tsps. ground coriander seeds
½ tsp. turmeric
2 tsps. mango powder
15 ml lemon juice
2 fresh green chillis, sliced lengthwise
1 tsp. chaat masala
½ tsp. black salt
Sliced red onions, for garnish
Fresh coriander leaves, roughly chopped, for garnish

DIRECTIONS:

1. Wash the chickpeas and set them aside to drain.
2. Heat the oil in a frying pan (or in the slow cooker if you have a sear setting). Add the cumin seeds, bay leaves, and cassia bark, and cook until fragrant, about 1 minute.
3. Stir in the sliced onions and salt, and cook for 5 to 6 minutes. Add the ginger, garlic, and chopped chillis and stir for 1 to 2 minutes.
4. Transfer to the slow cooker. Then add the chickpeas, tomatoes, chilli powder, ground coriander seeds, turmeric, mango powder, black salt, and hot water.
5. Cover and cook for 10 hours on low, or for 8 hours on high.
6. Leave the cooker on warm until ready to serve. Then top with sliced red onions, freshly chopped coriander leaves, sliced green chillis, and a sprinkle of chaat masala.

Lemon-Herb Pearl Barley Risotto

Prep time: 10 minutes
Cook time: 6 to 8 hours

INGREDIENTS:

1 tsp. extra-virgin olive oil
20 g minced onion
2 tbsps. minced preserved lemon
1 tsp. fresh thyme leaves
10 g roughly chopped fresh parsley, divided

175 g pearl barley
500 ml low-sodium vegetable broth
⅛ tsp. sea salt
Freshly ground black pepper, to taste
½ lemon, cut into wedges, for garnish

DIRECTIONS:

1. Grease the inside of the slow cooker with olive oil. Add the onion, preserved lemon, thyme, 2 tbsps. of the parsley, barley, and vegetable broth. Season with the salt and pepper, and stir thoroughly.
2. Cover and cook on low for 6 to 8 hours, until the barley is tender and all the liquid is absorbed. Garnish each serving with the remaining parsley and a lemon wedge.

Chilli Mexican Pinto Beans

Prep time: 20 minutes

Cook time: 8 to 9 hours

INGREDIENTS:

30 ml extra-virgin olive oil, divided

1.2 L water, plus extra as needed

450 g dried pinto beans, picked over and rinsed

235 ml mild lager, such as Budweiser

1 onion, finely chopped

4 garlic cloves, minced

1 tbsp. minced fresh oregano or 1 tsp. dried

1 tbsp. chilli powder

2 tsps. chipotle chilli pasta

Salt and pepper, to taste

2 tbsps. minced fresh coriander

10 g brown sugar

15 ml lime juice, plus extra for seasoning

DIRECTIONS:

1. Microwave onion, 15 ml oil, garlic, oregano, chilli powder, chipotle, and 1 tsp. salt in a bowl, stirring occasionally, until onion is softened, about 5 minutes. Transfer to a slow cooker. Stir in water, beans, and beer. Cover and cook until beans are tender, 8 to 9 hours on high.

2. Drain beans, reserving 235 ml cooking liquid. Return beans and reserved cooking liquid to the slow cooker. Stir in coriander, sugar, lime juice, and remaining 15 ml oil. Season with salt, pepper, and extra lime juice to taste. Serve. (Beans can be held on warm or low setting for up to 2 hours; adjust consistency with extra hot water as needed before serving.)

Red Lentil Dhal with Tomatoes

Prep time: 15 minutes

Cook time: 2 hours

INGREDIENTS:

15 g ghee or rapeseed oil

400 g red lentils, rinsed

950 ml hot water

1 small onion, chopped

1 tsp. salt, plus more as needed

1 bay leaf

3 garlic cloves, chopped

2 tomatoes, finely chopped

1 tsp. freshly grated ginger

1 tsp. turmeric

1 or 2 fresh green chillis, finely chopped

1 tsp. cumin seeds

1 dried red chilli

1 tsp. dried fenugreek leaves

1 tsp. garam masala

Chopped fresh coriander leaves, for garnish

DIRECTIONS:

1. Place the lentils, onion, salt, bay leaf, garlic, tomatoes, ginger, turmeric, chillis, and hot water into the slow cooker. Cover and cook on high for 2 hours, or on low for 4 hours.

2. Heat the ghee or rapeseed oil in a frying pan and add the cumin seeds. Cook until fragrant, about 1 minute. Then add the whole dried chilli. Toast for a second, then pour into the cooked lentils. Stir in the fenugreek and garam masala.

3. Check the seasoning, and if required, add a little salt. Top with a pinch of coriander leaves to serve. If you prefer your dhal a little thicker, leave it to simmer with the lid off until it has thickened.

Garlicky White Beans with Sage

Prep time: 10 minutes
Cook time: 8 to 9 hours

INGREDIENTS:
45 ml extra-virgin olive oil, divided
1 onion, finely chopped
5 garlic cloves, minced
700 ml vegetable or chicken broth, plus extra as needed
700 ml water
450 g dried small white beans, picked over and rinsed
2 tsps. minced fresh sage, divided
Salt and pepper, to taste

DIRECTIONS:
1. Microwave onion, garlic, 15 ml oil, 1 tsp. sage, and 1 tsp. salt in a bowl, stirring occasionally, until onion is softened, about 5 minutes. Transfer to a slow cooker. Stir in broth, water, and beans. Cover and cook until beans are tender, 8 to 9 hours on high.
2. Drain beans, reserving 235 ml cooking liquid. Return one-third of beans and reserved cooking liquid to the slow cooker and mash with potato masher until smooth. Stir in remaining beans, remaining 30 ml oil, and remaining 1 tsp. sage. Season with salt and pepper to taste. Serve. (Beans can be held on warm or low setting for up to 2 hours; adjust consistency with extra hot broth as needed before serving.)

Slow Cooker Refried Beans with Bacon

Prep time: 15 minutes
Cook time: 8 to 9 hours

INGREDIENTS:
450 g dried pinto beans, picked over and rinsed
1.5 L chicken broth, plus extra as needed
1 onion, finely chopped
1 poblano chilli, stemmed, deseeded, and minced
2 slices bacon
3 garlic cloves, minced
1 tbsp. ground cumin
3 tbsps. minced fresh coriander
15 ml lime juice, plus extra as needed
Salt and pepper, to taste

DIRECTIONS:
1. Microwave onion, poblano, bacon, garlic, and cumin in a bowl, stirring occasionally, until vegetables are softened, about 5 minutes. Transfer to a slow cooker. Stir in beans and broth, cover, and cook until beans are tender, 8 to 9 hours on high.
2. Discard bacon. Drain beans, reserving 235 ml cooking liquid. Return beans and reserved cooking liquid to the slow cooker and mash with potato masher until smooth. Stir in coriander, lime juice, and ½ tsp. salt. Season with salt, pepper, and extra lime juice to taste. Serve. (Beans can be held on warm or low setting for up to 2 hours; adjust consistency with extra hot broth as needed before serving.)

Braised Lentils with Escarole

Prep time: 10 minutes

Cook time: 3 to 4 hours

INGREDIENTS:
45 ml extra-virgin olive oil, divided
1 head endive (450 g), trimmed and sliced 2-cm thick
585 ml vegetable or chicken broth
200 g French green lentils, picked over and rinsed
1 onion, finely chopped
3 garlic cloves, minced
½ tsp. red pepper flakes
30 g Parmesan cheese, grated
15 ml lemon juice, plus extra for seasoning
Salt and pepper, to taste

DIRECTIONS:

1. Microwave onion, 15 ml oil, garlic, and pepper flakes in a bowl, stirring occasionally, until onion is softened, about 5 minutes. Transfer to a slow cooker. Stir in broth and lentils, cover, and cook until lentils are tender, 3 to 4 hours on low or 2 to 3 hours on high.
2. Stir in endive, 1 handful at a time, until slightly wilted. Cover and cook on high until chicory is completely wilted, about 10 minutes. Stir in Parmesan, lemon juice, and remaining oil. Season with salt, pepper, and extra lemon juice to taste. Serve.

White Beans with Pancetta and Carrot

Serve: 4

Prep time: 15 minutes

Cook time: 3½ to 4½ hours

INGREDIENTS:
60 ml olive oil
250 g dried cannellini beans
2 ribs celery, halved
400 g tinned chicken broth
A few slices of pancetta or prosciutto, chopped
3 shallots, halved
1 medium-size carrot, quartered
1 bay leaf
Sprig of fresh thyme or savoury
Fine sea salt and freshly ground black pepper, to taste
115 g fresh goat cheese, such as Chabis or Montrachet, crumbled
90 g sliced pitted black olives, or your choice, drained

DIRECTIONS:

1. Put the beans in a colander and rinse under cold running water, picking over for damaged beans and small stones. Transfer to the slow cooker and cover by 8 cm with cold water. Soak for 6 to 12 hours, drain, and add back to the cooker.
2. In a medium-size frying pan over medium-high heat, cook the pancetta in the olive oil, stirring, for 8 minutes. Add the shallots, carrot, and celery and cook, stirring, until just softened. Transfer the mixture to the beans in the cooker along with the bay leaf and herb sprig. Add the broth and enough water to cover the beans by 5 cm.
3. Cover and cook on high for 3½ to 4½ hours. The beans need to be covered with liquid at all times to cook properly. Toward the end of cooking, season with salt and pepper. When done, the beans will be tender and hold their shape, rather than fall apart. Remove the bay leaf and herb sprig and discard.
4. Serve the beans in soup bowls, topped with the crumbled goat cheese and sliced olives.

Chilli Yellow Mung Beans

Prep time: 10 minutes

Cook time: 2 hours

INGREDIENTS:

15 ml rapeseed oil
400 g yellow mung beans
5-cm piece fresh ginger, roughly chopped
80 ml water
1 lime, quartered
2 fresh green chillis
2 dried red chillis

1 tsp. mustard seeds
1 tsp. cumin seeds
1 bay leaf
1 tsp. chilli powder
1 tsp. turmeric
1 tsp. ground coriander seeds
1 tsp. salt

DIRECTIONS:

1. Wash the mung beans in several changes of water until the water runs clear. Drain the beans and leave them in the sieve.
2. In a mortar and pestle, pound the ginger with the green chillis to form a paste.
3. Heat the oil in a frying pan (or in the slow cooker if you have a sear setting). Add the mustard and cumin seeds. When they begin to crackle, add the dried red chillis, bay leaf, and ginger paste. Cook for a few seconds.
4. Transfer everything to the slow cooker. Add the yellow mung beans and mix.
5. Add the chilli powder, turmeric, coriander seeds, salt, and water, then stir.
6. Cover and cook on low for 2 hours, or on high for 1 hour. Serve with a squeeze of lime juice.

Cheese Pumpkin Polenta

Prep time: 10 minutes

Cook time: 3 to 3½ hours

INGREDIENTS:

235 ml evaporated milk
120 g coarse cornmeal
120 g mashed cooked pumpkin
120 g unsalted butter
60 g finely shredded Cheddar

cheese
350 ml water
1 tsp. salt
A few grinds of black pepper

DIRECTIONS:

1. Combine the cornmeal and some cold water in a bowl (the husks will rise to the top). Drain in a mesh strainer.
2. Combine the cornmeal, 350 ml of water, evaporated milk, and salt in the slow cooker. With a wooden or plastic spoon, stir for 15 seconds. Add the pumpkin and pepper, cover, and cook on high for 3 to 3½ hours or on low for 7 to 9 hours, until thick and creamy.
3. Stir in the butter and cheese, cover, turn off the cooker, and let the mixture rest for 10 minutes to melt the butter and cheese. Serve immediately.

Red Cannellini Bean Curry

Prep time: 15 minutes

Cook time: 8 hours

INGREDIENTS:

300 g dry red cannellini beans
950 ml hot water
200 g tinned plum tomatoes
1 onion, finely diced
2 tsps. freshly grated ginger
1 tsp. salt, plus more for seasoning
1 tsp. turmeric

4 garlic cloves, finely chopped
1 or 2 fresh green chillis, sliced
1 tsp. garam masala
Handful fresh coriander leaves, chopped
1 tsp. butter (optional)

DIRECTIONS:

1. Soak the cannellini beans overnight, then rinse. If you have a boil function on your slow cooker, cover the beans with water and boil for 10 minutes. If not, do this in a large pot. Drain and put the beans back into the slow cooker.
2. Add the remaining ingredients except the garam masala, coriander leaves, and butter. Cover and cook on low for 8 hours, or on high for 6 hours.
3. Add the garam masala, chopped coriander leaves, and butter (if using). Season with salt and serve.

CHAPTER 4
BEEF

Hearty Beef Roast

Prep time: 30 minutes
Cook time: 8 to 10 hours

INGREDIENTS:

15 ml olive oil
1 boneless beef chuck roast (1.5-1.8 kg)
900 g potatoes (about 6 medium), peeled and cut into 5-cm pieces
8 large fresh mushrooms, quartered
5 medium carrots (about 350 g), cut into 2½-cm pieces
400 g tinned diced tomatoes, undrained
2 celery ribs, chopped
1 medium onion, thinly sliced

15 g plain flour
35 g sliced Greek olives
30 g minced fresh parsley, divided
1 tbsp. minced fresh oregano or 1 tsp. dried oregano
15 ml lemon juice
2 tsps. minced fresh rosemary or ½ tsp. dried rosemary, crushed
2 garlic cloves, minced
¾ tsp. salt
¼ tsp. pepper
¼ tsp. crushed red pepper flakes (optional)

DIRECTIONS:

1. Place potatoes and carrots in a slow cooker. Sprinkle flour over all surfaces of roast. In a large frying pan, heat oil over medium-high heat. Brown roast on all sides. Place over vegetables.
2. Add mushrooms, celery, onion, olives and half of the parsley to slow cooker. In a small bowl, mix remaining ingredients; pour over top.
3. Cook, covered, on low 8 to 10 hours or until the meat and vegetables are tender. Remove beef. Stir remaining parsley into vegetables. Serve beef with vegetables.

Beef and Cabbage Stew

Prep time: 20 minutes
Cook time: 6 to 8 hours

INGREDIENTS:

225 g 90% lean beef mince
450 g tinned red beans, rinsed and drained
400 g tinned diced tomatoes, undrained
120 g shredded cabbage or angel hair coleslaw mix
230 g tomato passata
1 medium green pepper, chopped
175 ml salsa or picante sauce
1 small onion, chopped
3 garlic cloves, minced
1 tsp. ground cumin
½ tsp. pepper

DIRECTIONS:

1. In a large frying pan, cook beef over medium heat 4 to 6 minutes or until no longer pink, breaking into crumbles; drain.
2. Transfer meat to a slow cooker. Stir in remaining ingredients. Cook, covered, on low 6 to 8 hours or until cabbage is tender.

Braised Beef in Beer

Serve: 8 to 10

Prep time: 20 minutes

Cook time: 6 to 9 hours

INGREDIENTS:

1 (1¾ to 2½ kg) brisket or boneless chuck roast, trimmed off as much fat as possible and blotted dry

3 medium-size brown onions, cut in half and thinly sliced into half-moons

2 ribs celery, chopped

1 (340-g) bottle beer (not dark)

235 ml prepared chilli sauce

1 package dried onion soup mix

120 ml water

1 tsp. salt

¼ tsp. freshly ground black pepper

DIRECTIONS:

1. Put the roast in the slow cooker. If the meat is too big to lie flat in your cooker, cut it in half and stack the pieces one atop the other. Add the sliced onions and the celery.
2. In a medium-size bowl, combine the chilli sauce, beer, water, onion soup mix, salt, and pepper; pour it over the meat and vegetables. Cover and cook on low for 6 to 9 hours.
3. Skim off as much fat as possible from the sauce, slice the meat, and serve with the sauce.

Beef Short Ribs in Red Wine

Serve: 6

Prep time: 25 minutes

Cook time: 6¼ to 8¼ hours

INGREDIENTS:

15 g rapeseed oil

1.5 kg bone-in beef short ribs

4 medium carrots, cut into 2½-cm pieces

585 ml dry red wine or beef broth

2 large onions, cut into 1¼-cm wedges

235 ml beef broth

½ tsp. salt

½ tsp. pepper

4 fresh thyme sprigs

1 bay leaf

6 garlic cloves, minced

15 g tomato puree

4 tsps. cornflour

45 ml cold water

Salt and pepper, to taste

DIRECTIONS:

1. Sprinkle ribs with ½ tsp. each salt and pepper. In a large frying pan, heat oil over medium heat. In batches, brown ribs on all sides; transfer to a slow cooker. Add carrots, broth, thyme and bay leaf to ribs.
2. Add onions to the same frying pan; cook and stir over medium heat 8 to 9 minutes or until tender. Add garlic and tomato puree; cook and stir 1 minute longer. Stir in the wine. Bring to a boil; cook 8 to 10 minutes or until liquid is reduced by half. Add to the slow cooker. Cook, covered, on low 6 to 8 hours or until meat is tender.
3. Remove ribs and vegetables; keep warm. Transfer cooking juices to a small saucepan; skim fat. Discard thyme and bay leaf. Bring juices to a boil. In a small bowl, mix cornflour and water until smooth; stir into cooking juices. Return to a boil; cook and stir 1 to 2 minutes or until thickened. Season with salt and pepper to taste. Serve with ribs and vegetables.

Beef Ragoût and Veggies

Prep time: 25 minutes
Cook time: 7 to 8 hours

INGREDIENTS:

30 ml olive oil
900 g lean beef stew meat or beef cross rib roast, trimmed of fat, cut into 6-cm chunks, and blotted dry
2 large tomatoes, peeled, deseeded, and chopped, or 400 g tinned diced tomatoes, with their juice
2 medium-size onions, coarsely chopped
2 medium-size courgette, ends trimmed, cut in half lengthwise and sliced crosswise into ½-cm-thick half-moons
230 g fresh mushrooms, thickly sliced
235 ml dry red wine
75 g baby carrots
2 cloves garlic, minced
15 g quick-cooking tapioca
1 tsp. dried Italian herb seasoning
½ tsp. salt
¼ tsp. freshly ground black pepper

DIRECTIONS:

1. In a large frying pan over medium-high heat, heat 15 ml of the oil until very hot. Add half of the beef and brown on all sides, 3 to 4 minutes total. Transfer to the slow cooker. Add the remaining 15 ml of oil and brown the remaining beef.
2. Add the onions to the frying pan and brown slightly over medium-high heat. Add the tomatoes and wine and bring to a boil, scraping up any browned bits stuck to the pan; pour into the cooker. Add the carrots, garlic, tapioca, and Italian herbs to the cooker. Cover and cook on low for 6 to 7 hours.
3. Add the salt, pepper, courgette, and mushrooms, cover, turn the cooker to high, and cook for about 45 minutes, until the meat, mushrooms, and courgette are tender. Serve in shallow bowls or on rimmed dinner plates.

Garlicky Beef with Spring Onion

Prep time: 15 minutes
Cook time: 5 to 7 hours

INGREDIENTS:

60 ml sesame oil
1 beef sirloin tip roast (1.5 kg), thinly sliced
6 spring onions, sliced
100 g sugar
120 ml water
120 ml reduced-sodium soy sauce
45 g toasted sesame seeds
15 g plain flour
4 garlic cloves, minced
Additional sliced spring onions and toasted sesame seeds
Hot cooked rice, for serving

DIRECTIONS:

1. In a large resealable plastic bag, mix the first eight ingredients. Add beef; seal bag and turn to coat. Refrigerate 8 hours or overnight.
2. Pour beef and marinade into a slow cooker. Cook, covered, on low 5 to 7 hours or until meat is tender.
3. Using a slotted spoon, remove beef to a serving platter; sprinkle with additional spring onions and sesame seeds. Serve with rice.

Beef Burgundy with Mushroom

Serve: 6

Prep time: 25 minutes

Cook time: 7½ to 9½ hours

INGREDIENTS:
45 ml rapeseed oil
900 g beef sirloin tip steak, cubed
450 g sliced baby portobello mushrooms
235 ml Burgundy wine or beef broth
35 g plain flour
2 streaky bacon strips, diced
1½ tsps. minced fresh thyme or ½ tsp. dried thyme
¾ tsp. minced fresh marjoram or ¼ tsp. dried thyme
½ tsp. salt
½ tsp. seasoned salt
½ tsp. pepper
1 garlic clove, minced
1 tsp. beef stock granules
Hot cooked noodles, for serving (optional)

DIRECTIONS:

1. In a large resealable plastic bag, combine the first six ingredients. Add beef, a few pieces at a time, and shake to coat.
2. In a large frying pan, cook bacon over medium heat until crisp. Remove to kitchen towels with a slotted spoon; drain. In same frying pan, brown beef in oil in batches, adding garlic to the last batch; cook 1-2 minutes longer. Drain.
3. Transfer to a slow cooker. Add wine to frying pan, stirring to loosen browned bits from pan. Add stock; bring to a boil. Stir into a slow cooker. Stir in bacon. Cover and cook on low for 7 to 9 hours or until meat is tender.
4. Stir in mushrooms. Cover and cook on high 30 to 45 minutes longer or until mushrooms are tender and sauce is slightly thickened. Serve with noodles if desired.

Round Steak with Sweet Potato and Tomato

Serve: 6

Prep time: 20 minutes

Cook time: 7 to 9 hours

INGREDIENTS:
30 ml olive oil
2 beef top round steaks (450 g each)
900 g sweet potatoes, peeled and cut into 2½-cm pieces
800 g tinned diced tomatoes, undrained
1 large onion, chopped
1 medium green pepper, sliced
1 tsp. salt, divided
1 garlic clove, minced
20 g plain flour
120 ml beef broth
1 tsp. sugar
½ tsp. dried thyme
½ tsp. pepper
¼ tsp. hot pepper sauce

DIRECTIONS:

1. Place the sweet potatoes, onion and green pepper in a slow cooker. Cut each steak into three serving-size pieces; sprinkle with ½ tsp. salt. In a large frying pan over medium heat, brown steaks in oil in batches on both sides. Place steaks over vegetables, reserving drippings in a pan.
2. Add garlic to drippings; cook and stir for 1 minute. Stir in flour until blended. Stir in the remaining ingredients and remaining salt. Bring to a boil, stirring constantly. Cook and stir for 4 to 5 minutes or until thickened. Pour over meat. Cover and cook on low for 7 to 9 hours or until beef is tender.

Tangy Flank Steak Fajitas

Serve: 6

Prep time: 25 minutes

Cook time: 6 to 8 hours

INGREDIENTS:

175 ml prepared chunky salsa
15 g tomato puree
15 ml olive oil
1 clove garlic, minced
45 ml fresh lime juice
1 tsp. freshly ground black pepper
½ tsp. salt

For Serving:
Warm flour tortillas (the small ones)
245 g guacamole

1 (700 g) flank steak, trimmed of excess fat and silver skin
1 large white onion, cut in half and thinly sliced into half-moons
3 red peppers, deseeded and cut into ½-cm-wide strips

150 g chopped plum tomatoes
½ bunch fresh coriander, chopped

DIRECTIONS:

1. In a small bowl, combine salsa, tomato puree, olive oil, garlic, lime juice, pepper, and salt. Lay the flank steak in the slow cooker and pour the mixture over it, making sure to coat all exposed surfaces well. Lay the onion and red peppers on top. Cover and cook on low for 6 to 8 hours, until the meat is tender.
2. Remove the steak and vegetables from the juice and transfer to a serving platter. Cover with aluminium foil and let stand 10 minutes. Cut the meat across the grain into 1-cm-thick slices. Serve it heaped over warm tortillas, with the peppers and onions on top. Garnish with a dab of guacamole, some chopped tomatoes, and the coriander on top.

Cheesy Beef Stuffed Peppers

Serve: 4

Prep time: 15 minutes

Cook time: 5 to 6 hours

INGREDIENTS:

4 medium green or sweet red peppers
450 g beef mince
1 (249-g) package ready-to-serve Spanish rice
240 g shredded mild cheddar

cheese, divided
350 ml salsa
15 ml hot pepper sauce
235 ml water
2 tbsps. minced fresh coriander

DIRECTIONS:

1. Cut tops off peppers and remove seeds; set aside. In a large frying pan, cook beef over medium heat until no longer pink; drain.
2. Stir in the rice, ¾ of the cheese, salsa and pepper sauce. Spoon into peppers. Transfer to a slow cooker. Pour water around peppers.
3. Cover and cook on low for 5 to 6 hours or until peppers are tender and filling is heated through. Top with remaining cheese; sprinkle with coriander.

Vinegary Steak with Green Chillies

Serve: 4

Prep time: 20 minutes

Cook time: 6 to 8 hours

INGREDIENTS:

15 ml rapeseed oil
1 beef flank steak (700 g)
1 large onion, sliced
115 g tinned chopped green chillies
80 ml water

30 ml cider vinegar
2 to 3 tsps. chilli powder
1 tsp. garlic powder
1 tsp. sugar
½ tsp. salt
⅛ tsp. pepper

DIRECTIONS:

1. In a large frying pan, heat oil over medium-high heat; brown steak on both sides. Transfer to a slow cooker.
2. Add onion to same frying pan; cook and stir 1 to 2 minutes or until crisp-tender. Add water to pan; cook 30 seconds, stirring to loosen browned bits from pan. Stir in remaining ingredients; return to a boil. Pour over steak.
3. Cook, covered, on low 6 to 8 hours or until meat is tender. Slice steak across the grain; serve with onion mixture.

CHAPTER 5
PORK

Sweet and Spiced Pork Loin and Potatoes

Prep time: 25 minutes

Cook time: 4 to 5 hours

INGREDIENTS:

120 ml olive oil

1 (1¾ kg) pork loin roast, rolled and tied

2 medium sweet potatoes, peeled and cut into 2½-cm chunks or wedges

2 medium waxy potatoes, peeled and cut into 2½-cm chunks or wedges

2 medium red onions, cut into quarters

120 ml chicken broth

45 g brown sugar

1 tsp. ground cumin

1½ tsps. fennel seeds

½ tsp. ground cinnamon

½ tsp. ground ginger

2 tsps. salt

1 tsp. freshly ground black pepper

DIRECTIONS:

1. Arrange the vegetables in the insert of a slow cooker. Drizzle 60 ml of the oil over the vegetables and toss to coat. Combine the cumin, fennel seeds, cinnamon, ginger, sugar, salt, and pepper in a small bowl. Sprinkle 1 tbsp. of the rub over the vegetables and toss again.
2. Pat the rest of the rub over the meat, place the meat on the vegetables, and drizzle with the remaining olive oil. Pour in the chicken broth. Cover and cook on high for 4 to 5 hours or on low for 8 to 10 hours, until the pork and vegetables are tender. The roast should register 80°C on an instant-read thermometer.
3. Transfer the pork to a cutting board, cover with aluminium foil, and let rest for 20 minutes. Cut the meat into 1-cm-thick slices and arrange on the centre of a platter. Spoon the vegetables around the meat and serve.

Asian Braised Spareribs

Prep time: 5 minutes

Cook time: 8 to 10 hours

INGREDIENTS:

1.5 kg country-style spareribs

475 ml soy sauce

235 ml rice wine (mirin)

60 ml hoisin sauce

60 ml rice vinegar

30 g sugar

1 tsp. freshly grated ginger

DIRECTIONS:

1. Stir the soy sauce, rice wine, ginger, hoisin, rice vinegar, and sugar together in the insert of a slow cooker.
2. Add the ribs to the pot and spoon the liquid over the ribs. Cover and cook on low for 8 to 10 hours, until the ribs are tender. Skim off any fat from the sauce.
3. Serve the ribs from the cooker set on warm.

Country-Style Spareribs

Prep time: 10 minutes
Cook time: 8 to 10 hours

INGREDIENTS:
30 ml extra-virgin olive oil
1.5 kg country-style spareribs
120 ml red wine, such as Chianti or Barolo
800 g tinned crushed tomatoes, with their juice
3 medium onions, finely chopped
⅛ tsp. red pepper flakes
3 cloves garlic, minced
1 tsp. dried oregano
1½ tsps. salt

DIRECTIONS:
1. Sprinkle the ribs with the salt and arrange in the insert of a slow cooker. Heat the oil in a large frying pan over medium-high heat. Add the onions, red pepper flakes, garlic, and oregano and sauté until the onions are softened, about 5 minutes.
2. Add the wine to the frying pan and stir up any browned bits from the bottom of the pan. Transfer the contents of the frying pan to the slow-cooker insert and stir in the tomatoes. Cover and cook on low for 8 to 10 hours, until the meat is tender. Skim off any fat from the surface of the sauce.
3. Serve the ribs from the cooker set on warm.

Teriyaki Pork Tenderloin

Prep time: 5 minutes
Cook time: 3 hours

INGREDIENTS:
30 ml rapeseed oil
2 (450 g) pork tenderloins
235 ml soy sauce
60 ml rice vinegar
15 g light brown sugar
2 cloves garlic, minced
1 tsp. grated fresh ginger

DIRECTIONS:
1. Whisk the oil, garlic, ginger, soy sauce, vinegar, and sugar together in a bowl until blended. Remove the silver skin from the outside of the pork with a boning knife and discard.
2. Place the tenderloins in a 1-gallon zipper-top plastic bag or 23-by-33-cm baking dish. Pour the marinade over the tenderloins and seal the bag or cover the dish with cling film.
3. Marinate for at least 4 hours or overnight, turning the meat once or twice during that time. Place the marinade and pork in the insert of a slow cooker. Cover and cook on high for 3 hours.
4. Remove the meat from the sauce, cover loosely with aluminium foil, and allow the meat to rest for about 10 minutes. Skim off any fat from the top of the sauce.
5. Cut the meat diagonally in 1-cm-thick slices. Nap each serving of pork with some of the sauce.

Chilli Pork Chops and Peppers

Prep time: 25 minutes

Cook time: 3½ to 4 hours

INGREDIENTS:
60 ml olive oil
6 (2½-cm-thick) pork loin chops
2 medium onions, cut into half rounds
2 medium red peppers, deseeded and cut into 1¼-cm slices
2 medium yellow peppers, deseeded and cut into 1¼-cm slices
1 tsp. ground cumin
1 tsp. sugar
1 tsp. salt
½ tsp. freshly ground black pepper
800 g tinned crushed tomatoes, with their juice
1 tsp. ancho chilli powder

DIRECTIONS:
1. Heat 20 ml of the oil in a large frying pan over medium-high heat. Add the onions, peppers, cumin, sugar, salt, and pepper and sauté until the onions begin to turn translucent, about 10 minutes. Add the tomatoes and stir to combine. Transfer the mixture to the insert of a slow cooker. Cover the cooker and set on low.
2. Heat the remaining oil in the frying pan over medium-high heat. Sprinkle the chilli powder evenly over the chops and add to the frying pan. Brown the chops on all sides. Transfer the chops to the slow- cooker insert and spoon some of the sauce over the chops.
3. Cover the slow cooker and cook on high for 3½ to 4 hours or on low for 6 to 8 hours, until the pork is tender.
4. Serve the pork chops with the sauce.

Slow Cooker Pork and Black Beans

Prep time: 15 minutes

Cook time: 4½ to 5 hours

INGREDIENTS:
3 medium carrots, sliced
1 boneless pork shoulder butt roast (1.5-1.8 kg)
400 g tinned black beans, rinsed and drained
280 g green enchilada sauce
10 g minced fresh coriander
60 ml cold water
1 tbsp. cornflour
Hot cooked rice, for serving

DIRECTIONS:
1. Place carrots in a slow cooker. Cut roast in half; place in slow cooker. Add the beans, enchilada sauce and coriander. Cover and cook on low for 4½ to 5 hours or until a meat thermometer reads 70ºC. Remove roast to a serving platter; keep warm.
2. Skim fat from cooking juices. Transfer the cooking liquid, carrots and beans to a small saucepan. Bring to a boil. Combine cornflour and water until smooth. Gradually stir into the pan. Bring to a boil; cook and stir for 2 minutes or until thickened. Serve with meat and rice.

Pork Chops with Plum Sauce

Prep time: 10 minutes
Cook time: 3½ to 4 hours

INGREDIENTS:
60 ml olive oil
6 (2½-cm-thick) pork loin chops
240 g plum jam
2 medium onions, finely chopped
120 g ketchup
30 g Dijon mustard
30 ml fresh lemon juice
Grated zest of 1 lemon
1 tsp. salt
½ tsp. freshly ground black pepper

DIRECTIONS:
1. Heat the oil in a large frying pan over high heat. Sprinkle the salt and pepper evenly over the pork chops and add to the frying pan. Brown the pork on all sides.
2. Transfer to the insert of a slow cooker. lower heat to medium-high. Add the onions to the frying pan and sauté until the onions are softened, about 3 to 5 minutes. Add the plum jam to the frying pan and scrape up any browned bits from the bottom of the pan. Transfer the contents of the frying pan to the slow-cooker insert.
3. Add the mustard, lemon juice and zest, and ketchup and stir to combine. Cover and cook on high for 3½ to 4 hours or on low for 6 to 8 hours. Skim off any fat from the surface of the sauce.
4. Serve the pork chops from the slow cooker set on warm.

Braised Pork Loin in Cider

Prep time: 20 minutes
Cook time: 4 hours

INGREDIENTS:
30 ml olive oil
1 (1 to 1.5 kg) pork loin roast, rolled and tied
120 ml sweet apple cider or apple juice
235 ml beef stock
4 large Gala apples, peeled, cored, and cut into 8 wedges each
120 g Dijon mustard
85 g light brown sugar
1 large onion, finely sliced
2 tsps. dried thyme
175 ml double cream
Salt and freshly ground black pepper, to taste
450 g buttered cooked wide egg noodles, for serving

DIRECTIONS:
1. Heat the oil in a large sauté pan over medium-high heat. Make a paste of the mustard and sugar and spread over the roast on all sides. Add the roast to the pan and brown on all sides. Add the onion and thyme to the sauté pan and cook until the onion is softened, 3 to 5 minutes.
2. Transfer the roast, onion, and any bits from the bottom of the pan to the insert of a slow cooker. Add the cider and beef stock. Cover the slow cooker and cook on high for 3 hours. Remove the cover and add the apples and cream. Cover and cook on high for an additional 1 hour.
3. Remove the pork from the slow-cooker insert, cover with aluminium foil, and allow to rest for 15 minutes. Season the sauce with salt and pepper. Remove the strings from the roast, cut into thin slices, and serve the pork on the buttered noodles, napping both with some of the sauce.

Maple Pork Chops in Bourbon

Serve: 6

Prep time: 10 minutes

Cook time: 3 to 4 hours

INGREDIENTS:

30 g unsalted butter
30 ml olive oil
6 (2½-cm-thick) pork loin chops
2 medium onions, finely chopped
120 ml pure maple syrup
120 g ketchup

120 ml bourbon
120 ml beef broth
1 tsp. Tabasco sauce
1 tsp. dry mustard
1½ tsps. salt
½ tsp. freshly ground black pepper

DIRECTIONS:

1. Heat the oil in a large frying pan over high heat. Sprinkle the salt and pepper evenly over the pork chops and add to the frying pan.
2. Brown the chops on both sides, adding a few at a time, being careful not to crowd the pan, and transfer to the insert of a slow cooker.
3. Melt the butter in the frying pan over medium-high heat. Add the onions and sauté until they begin to soften, about 5 minutes. Add the remaining ingredients and scrape up any browned bits from the bottom of the pan. Transfer the contents of the frying pan to the slow-cooker insert.
4. Cover and cook on high for 3 to 4 hours or on low for 6 to 8 hours. Skim off any fat from the top of the sauce.
5. Serve from the cooker set on warm.

Pork Ribs with Peach Sauce

Serve: 4

Prep time: 20 minutes

Cook time: 5½ to 6½ hours

INGREDIENTS:

900 g boneless country-style pork ribs
120 ml mild salsa
150 g chopped fresh peeled peaches or frozen unsweetened

sliced peaches, thawed and chopped
60 g peach jam
60 ml barbecue sauce
2 tbsps. taco seasoning

DIRECTIONS:

1. In a large bowl, toss pork ribs with taco seasoning. Cover and refrigerate overnight.
2. Place pork in a slow cooker. In a small bowl, combine the salsa, peach jam and barbecue sauce. Pour over ribs. Cover and cook on low for 5 to 6 hours or until meat is tender.
3. Add peaches; cover and cook 30 minutes longer or until peaches are tender.

Asian BBQ Pork Loin Back Ribs

Serve: 6

Prep time: 10 minutes

Cook time: 7½ to 8½ hours

INGREDIENTS:

1 tbsp. toasted sesame oil
1¾ kg pork loin back ribs (about 3 slabs), cut to fit the slow cooker
120 ml soy sauce
120 ml chicken broth
60 ml hoisin sauce

45 g brown sugar
2 tsps. grated fresh ginger
2 cloves garlic, minced
4 spring onions, finely chopped, using the white and tender green parts

DIRECTIONS:

1. Stir the soy sauce, hoisin, ginger, garlic, sugar, sesame oil, broth, and spring onions together in the insert of a slow cooker. Add the ribs and push them down into the sauce.
2. Cover and cook on low for 7 to 8 hours, until the meat is tender. Remove cover and cook for an additional 30 to 35 minutes.
3. Serve the ribs with the remaining sauce on the side.

CHAPTER 6
LAMB

Indian Tandoori Lamb

Prep time: 20 minutes

Cook time: 3 hours

INGREDIENTS:

1.5 kg lamb shoulder, fat trimmed and cut into 2½-cm chunks

4 medium waxy potatoes, cut into quarters

3 medium carrots, cut into 2½-cm lengths

375 g plain yoghurt

120 ml chicken broth

30 ml fresh lemon juice

4 cloves garlic, minced

1½ tsps. ground cumin

1½ tsps. garam masala

1 tsp. ground coriander

Pinch of cayenne pepper

1 tsp. salt

DIRECTIONS:

1. Whisk together the yoghurt, lemon juice, garlic, and spices in a large bowl. Add the lamb and toss to coat well with the marinade. Cover and refrigerate for at least 2 hours or overnight.
2. Drain the marinade and add the lamb to the insert of a slow cooker. Add the vegetables and broth and stir to combine. Cover and cook on high for 3 hours, until the lamb is tender and the vegetables are cooked through. Skim off any fat from the top of the sauce.
3. Serve from the cooker set on warm.

Braised Lamb with Aubergine

Prep time: 25 minutes

Cook time: 3 to 4 hours

INGREDIENTS:

60 ml extra-virgin olive oil

1.5 kg lamb shoulder, fat trimmed and cut into 2½-cm chunks

4 Japanese aubergines (about 450 g), cut into 1¼-cm cubes

800g tinned chopped tomatoes, with their juice

2 large onions, coarsely chopped

120 ml dry white wine or vermouth

1½ tsps. salt

½ tsp. freshly ground black pepper

4 cloves garlic, sliced

1 tsp. dried oregano

15 g finely chopped fresh Italian parsley

75 g crumbled feta cheese, for garnish

DIRECTIONS:

1. Heat the oil in a large frying pan over medium-high heat. Sprinkle the lamb evenly with the salt and pepper, add a few pieces at a time to the frying pan, and brown on all sides. Transfer the browned meat to the insert of a slow cooker.
2. Add the onions, garlic, aubergines, and oregano to the frying pan and sauté until the onions begin to soften and turn translucent, 5 to 7 minutes. Add the wine to the frying pan and heat, scraping the browned bits from the bottom of the pan. Transfer the contents of the frying pan to the slow-cooker insert and stir in the tomatoes.
3. Cover and cook on high 3 to 4 hours or low for 7 to 8 hours. Skim off any fat from the top of the stew and stir in the parsley. Keep the stew in the cooker set on warm until ready to serve.
4. Garnish each serving with a sprinkling of feta.

Lemony Lamb with Artichokes

Prep time: 20 minutes

Cook time: 8 hours

INGREDIENTS:

120 ml olive oil
1½ tsps. salt
1 tsp. ground cumin
Pinch of cayenne pepper
1 tsp. sweet paprika
1.5 kg lamb shoulder meat, fat trimmed and cut into 2½-cm chunks
4 leeks, cut into 1¼-cm pieces, using the white and tender green parts
4 garlic cloves, minced
235 ml dry white wine
120 ml chicken broth
Grated zest of 2 lemons
450 g frozen artichoke hearts, thawed and drained

DIRECTIONS:

1. Mix 60 ml of the oil, the salt, cumin, cayenne, and paprika in a large bow. Add the meat and toss to coat with the spice mixture. Heat the remaining oil in a large frying pan over medium-high heat. Add the meat a few pieces at a time and brown on all sides. Transfer the browned meat to the insert of a slow cooker.
2. Add the leeks and garlic to the same frying pan and sauté until the leeks are softened, 3 to 4 minutes. Add the wine, broth, and zest and heat, scraping up any browned bits from the bottom of the pan.
3. Pour the contents of the frying pan over the lamb and add the artichokes, stirring to distribute the ingredients in the pot. Cover and cook on low for 8 hours, until the lamb is tender.
4. Using a slotted spoon, carefully transfer the lamb and artichokes to a serving bowl. Strain the sauce through a fine-mesh sieve into a saucepan. Skim off any fat from the top and bring to a boil. Boil until the sauce is reduced to about 350 ml to concentrate the flavour. Taste and adjust the seasoning.
5. Spoon the sauce over the lamb and artichokes and serve.

Lemony Leg of Lamb

Prep time: 10 minutes

Cook time: 3 to 4 hours

INGREDIENTS:

120 g Dijon mustard
60 ml fresh lemon juice
Grated zest of 2 lemons
6 garlic cloves, minced
60 ml extra-virgin olive oil
1 tsp. dried oregano
1 tsp. salt
½ tsp. freshly ground black pepper
1 (1.5-1.8 kg) boneless leg of lamb, butterflied, fat trimmed
235 ml dry white wine
15 g finely chopped fresh Italian parsley

DIRECTIONS:

1. Combine the mustard, lemon juice, zest, garlic, oil, oregano, salt, and pepper in a mixing bowl. Pour the marinade into a zipper-top plastic bag, add the lamb to the bag, and turn it to coat. Seal the bag and refrigerate for at least 8 hours or up to 24 hours.
2. Drain the marinade, and roll the meat into a compact cylinder, tying the meat at 2½-cm intervals with kitchen string or silicone loops, and put the lamb in insert of a slow cooker. Add the wine. Cover and cook on high for 3 to 4 hours, until the meat is tender. Remove the meat from the slow cooker, cover with aluminium foil, and allow to rest for 20 minutes.
3. Strain the sauce through a fine-mesh sieve into a saucepan and remove any fat from the surface. Boil until the sauce is reduced by half. Taste and adjust the seasonings, adding the parsley to the sauce.
4. Cut the meat into 1-cm-thick slices and serve with the sauce on the side.

Lamb and Vegetables Stew

Prep time: 20 minutes
Cook time: 7 to 9 hours

INGREDIENTS:

30 ml olive oil
680 g lamb stew meat, cubed
2 shallots, sliced
120 ml red wine
800 ml beef broth
2 medium potatoes, cubed
2 large carrots, cut into 2½-cm pieces
2 medium parsnips, peeled and cubed
1 large sweet potato, peeled and cubed
4 streaky bacon strips, cooked and crumbled
70 g plain flour
½ tsp. salt
¼ tsp. pepper
1 garlic clove, minced
1 tbsp. mint sauce

DIRECTIONS:

1. In a large resealable plastic bag, combine the flour, salt and pepper. Add the meat, a few pieces at a time, and shake to coat. In a large frying pan, brown meat and shallots in oil in batches.
2. Transfer to a slow cooker. Add wine to the frying pan, stirring to loosen browned bits from pan. Bring to a boil. Reduce heat; simmer, uncovered, for 1-2 minutes. Add to a slow cooker.
3. Stir in the broth, potatoes, sweet potato, carrots, parsnips and garlic. Cover and cook on low for 7 to 9 hours or until meat is tender. Stir in mint sauce; sprinkle with bacon.

Guinness Lamb Shanks and Parsnip

Prep time: 20 minutes
Cook time: 10 to 12 hours

INGREDIENTS:

60 ml olive oil
6 meaty lamb shanks, fat trimmed (lamb shanks range in size from 350 to 450 g, depending on the size of the bone)
3 large onions, cut into half rounds
1 (340-g) bottle Guinness or other dark ale
4 medium carrots, cut into 2½-cm lengths
4 medium parsnips, cut into 2½-cm lengths
120 ml beef broth
70 g plain flour
30 g tomato puree
1½ tsps. salt
½ tsp. freshly ground black pepper

DIRECTIONS:

1. Mix the flour, salt, and pepper in a large zipper-top plastic bag. Add the meat, toss to coat, and shake off any excess flour. Heat the oil in a large frying pan over high heat. Add the meat a few pieces at a time and brown on all sides. Transfer the browned meat to the insert of a slow cooker.
2. Add the onions to the same frying pan and sauté until they begin to soften and turn translucent, 4 to 5 minutes. Pour in the Guinness and scrape up any browned bits from the bottom of the pan.
3. Transfer the contents of the frying pan to the slow-cooker insert, add the carrots and parsnips, and stir to distribute evenly. Stir the tomato puree into the broth and pour into the insert. Cover and cook on low for 10 to 12 hours, until the meat is tender. Skim off any fat from the top of the sauce.
4. Serve the lamb directly from the cooker set on warm.

Braised Lamb Chops and White Beans

Prep time: 20 minutes

Cook time: 5 to 7 hours

INGREDIENTS:
15 to 30 ml olive oil
4 shoulder lamb chops
400 g tinned small white beans, rinsed and drained
1 medium-size brown onion, chopped
120 ml chicken broth
120 ml dry white wine
15 g chopped oil-packed sun-dried tomatoes, drained
½ tsp. dried marjoram or thyme
Pinch of ground cumin
Salt and freshly ground black pepper, to taste
Hot cooked rice, for serving

DIRECTIONS:
1. In a large non-stick frying pan, heat the oil and brown the lamb on both sides over medium-high heat; transfer to the slow cooker. Add the onion to the frying pan and cook for a few minutes until limp; add to the cooker. Add the broth, wine, tomatoes, marjoram, and cumin, cover, and cook on low for 2½ to 3½ hours.
2. Add the beans, cover, and continue to cook on low until the lamb is very tender, another 2½ to 3½ hours. Season with salt and pepper and serve over rice.

Lamb Cassoulet with White Beans

Prep time: 25 minutes

Cook time: 6½ to 8½ hours

INGREDIENTS:
120 ml extra-virgin olive oil
6 meaty lamb shanks, fat trimmed
450 g dried white beans, soaked overnight and drained
3 medium onions, coarsely chopped
4 cloves garlic, minced
4 medium carrots, coarsely chopped
4 celery sticks, coarsely chopped
800 g tinned crushed tomatoes, with their juice
1.2 L chicken broth
700 ml beef broth
1½ tsps. salt
½ tsp. freshly ground black pepper
1 tbsp. fresh rosemary leaves, finely chopped
1 bay leaf
For the Topping:
100 g fresh bread crumbs
60 g freshly grated Parmigiano-Reggiano cheese
4 cloves garlic, minced
15 g finely chopped fresh Italian parsley

DIRECTIONS:
1. Place the beans in the insert of a slow cooker. Heat the oil in a large frying pan over medium-high heat. Sprinkle the meat evenly with the salt and pepper. Add as many lamb shanks as will fit in a single layer and brown on all sides. Transfer the browned shanks to the slow-cooker insert. Brown any remaining shanks and transfer them to the slow cooker insert.
2. Add the onions, garlic, carrots, celery, and rosemary to the same frying pan and sauté until the vegetables are softened, 5 to 7 minutes. Add the tomatoes and 235 ml of the chicken broth to the frying pan and heat, scraping up any browned bits from the bottom of the pan. Transfer the tomato mixture to the slow cooker insert and stir in the remaining broths, and the bay leaf. Cover and cook on high for 6 to 8 hours or low for 10 to 12 hours, until the beans and lamb are tender.
3. Combine all the ingredients for the topping in a small bowl while the lamb is cooking. Cover and refrigerate.
4. Uncover the cooker and spoon off any fat on the surface. Taste and adjust with the seasoning. Sprinkle the topping over the cassoulet, cover, and cook on high another 30 minutes.
5. Serve the cassoulet from the cooker set on warm.

Guinness-Glazed Lamb Shanks

Serve: 4

Prep time: 25 minutes

Cook time: 6 to 8 hours

INGREDIENTS:

60 ml olive oil, divided
4 lamb shanks (about 565 g each)
900 g waxy potatoes, peeled and
cut into chunks
235 ml lemon juice
4 garlic cloves, thinly sliced
1 tbsp. each minced fresh
thyme, rosemary and parsley
1 tsp. salt
½ tsp. pepper

For the Sauce:
235 ml Guinness (dark beer)
85 g honey
3 fresh thyme sprigs
2 bay leaves
15 g Dijon mustard
2 garlic cloves, minced
½ tsp. salt
¼ tsp. pepper
⅛ tsp. crushed red pepper flakes

DIRECTIONS:

1. Cut slits into each lamb shank; insert garlic slices. In a large resealable plastic bag, combine the lemon juice, 30 ml oil, thyme, rosemary, parsley, salt and pepper. Add the lamb; seal bag and turn to coat. Refrigerate overnight.
2. Drain and discard marinade. In a large frying pan, brown shanks in remaining oil on all sides in batches. Place shanks in a slow cooker.
3. In the same frying pan, combine the beer, honey, thyme, bay leaves, Dijon, garlic, salt, pepper and pepper flakes. Bring to a boil, stirring constantly. Pour over meat. Cover and cook on low for 6-8 hours or until meat and potatoes are tender, adding the potatoes during the last 2 hours of cooking.
4. Remove lamb and potatoes from the slow cooker. Strain sauce and discard bay leaves. If desired, thicken sauce. Serve with lamb and potatoes.

Lamb Leg with Mint Pesto

Serve: 8

Prep time: 20 minutes

Cook time: 8 to 10 hours

INGREDIENTS:

1 (1.5-1.8 kg) leg of lamb, boned and butterflied
2 large onions, cut into half rounds
235 ml beef broth
235 ml dry white wine
For the Mint Pesto:
60 ml olive oil
30 g packed fresh mint leaves
6 or 7 leaves fresh oregano
4 cloves garlic
15 ml rice vinegar or white vinegar
1 tsp. salt
⅛ tsp. cayenne pepper

DIRECTIONS:

1. Put all the pesto ingredients in a food processor or blender and process until the ingredients are a paste. Cover and refrigerate for up to 4 days.
2. Spread the onions over the bottom of the insert of a slow cooker. Pour in the wine and beef broth. Lay the lamb, fat-side down, boned-side up on a cutting board or flat surface and spread all the pesto over the surface of the lamb.
3. Roll up the meat, starting from the short end, and tie with kitchen string or silicone loops. Arrange on top of the onions in the slow-cooker insert. Cover and cook on low for 8 to 10 hours, until the lamb is tender. Remove the lamb from the slow-cooker insert, cover with aluminium foil, and allow to rest for 20 minutes.
4. Strain the sauce through a fine-mesh sieve into a saucepan and remove any fat from the surface. Boil the sauce until it is reduced by about one quarter, 10 to 15 minutes.
5. Remove the strings from the lamb, cut into 1-cm-thick slices, and serve with the sauce on the side.

CHAPTER 7
POULTRY

Cheddar Chicken Enchiladas

Prep time: 10 minutes
Cook time: 2 hours

INGREDIENTS:
15 ml rapeseed oil
675 to 900 g tinned green chilli enchilada sauce
350 to 450 g cooked boneless, skinless chicken, cut into 2-cm pieces
1 large brown onion, chopped
500 g shredded mild cheddar
500 g soured cream (reduced fat is okay)
1 dozen soft corn tortillas, each one cut into 4 strips

DIRECTIONS:
1. In a large frying pan, heat the oil over medium-high heat, then add the onion and cook, stirring, until softened, about 5 minutes. Set aside.
2. Pour about 115 ml of the enchilada sauce into the slow cooker; tilt to spread it around. In layers, add one-quarter of the tortilla strips, one-quarter of the remaining sauce, one-third of the sautéed onion, one-third of the chicken, and one-quarter of the cheese. Repeat the layers two more times, ending with the cheese. Finish the bake with the remaining tortilla strips, sauce, and cheese.
3. Spoon the soured cream over the surface of the bake in big dollops. Use a spatula or the back of a large spoon to gently spread it all around without disturbing the layers. Cover and cook on high for 2 hours, or on low for 4 to 5 hours.
4. To serve, use a long-handled spoon to reach down through all the layers for each serving. Make sure each diner gets some of the soured cream.

Peach Glazed Chicken Thighs

Prep time: 15 minutes
Cook time: 4 to 5 hours

INGREDIENTS:
10 boneless skinless chicken thighs (about 1 kg)
75 g sliced peeled fresh or frozen peaches
235 ml peach jam
75 ml chilli sauce
160 g sultanas
15 ml reduced-sodium soy sauce
2 tbsps. minced crystallized ginger
1 tbsp. minced garlic
Hot cooked rice (optional)

DIRECTIONS:
1. Place chicken in a slow cooker coated with cooking spray. Top with peaches and sultanas. In a small bowl, combine the peach jam, chilli sauce, ginger, soy sauce and garlic. Spoon over the top.
2. Cover and cook on low for 4 to 5 hours or until chicken is tender. Serve with rice if desired.

Jerk Chicken

Prep time: 5 minutes

Cook time: 2½ to 3 hours

INGREDIENTS:

8 chicken breast halves, skin and bones removed

350 ml mango nectar

85 g light brown sugar

30 g dark corn syrup

30 ml rice vinegar

2 tsps. jerk seasoning

DIRECTIONS:

1. Add the jerk seasoning, nectar, sugar, corn syrup, and rice vinegar to the insert of a slow cooker and stir to combine.
2. Add the chicken breasts and turn to coat in the sauce. Cover and cook on high for 2½ to 3 hours, until the chicken is cooked through.
3. Serve the chicken hot, warm, or at room temperature.

Chicken Cacciatore with Mushroom

Prep time: 10 minutes

Cook time: 4½ to 5½ hours

INGREDIENTS:

60 ml extra-virgin olive oil

10 chicken thighs, skin and bones removed

800 g tinned crushed tomatoes, with their juice

450 g chestnut mushrooms, quartered

15 g dried cep mushrooms, crumbled

60 ml red wine

2 tsps. salt

Pinch red pepper flakes

1 tsp. dried oregano

3 cloves garlic, minced

DIRECTIONS:

1. Heat 30 ml of the oil in a large frying pan over high heat. Add the mushrooms, 1 tsp. of the salt, red pepper flakes, oregano, and garlic and sauté until the liquid in the pan has evaporated, about 7 to 10 minutes.
2. Add the ceps and the wine to a small bowl and allow the cep to soften. Add the wine mixture and the tomatoes to the frying pan.
3. Transfer the contents of the pan to the insert of a slow cooker.
4. Sprinkle the chicken evenly with the remaining 1 tsp. salt. Heat the remaining 30 ml oil in the same frying pan over high heat. Add the chicken to the frying pan and brown on all sides, 15 to 20 minutes.
5. Transfer the browned meat to the slow-cooker insert, submerging it in the sauce. Cover and cook on low for 4 to 5 hours, until the chicken is tender and cooked through. Skim off any fat from the top of the sauce.
6. Serve from the cooker set on warm.

Pot-Roast Turkey Drumsticks

Serve: 3

Prep time: 20 minutes

Cook time: 5 to 5½ hours

INGREDIENTS:

3 turkey drumsticks (350 g each), skin removed

3 medium potatoes, peeled and quartered

2 celery ribs, cut into 6-cm pieces

150 g fresh baby carrots

1 medium onion, peeled and quartered

3 garlic cloves, peeled and quartered

120 ml chicken broth

2 tsps. seasoned salt

1 tsp. dried thyme

1 tsp. dried parsley flakes

¼ tsp. pepper

DIRECTIONS:

1. In a greased slow cooker, combine the first six ingredients. Place drumsticks over vegetables. Sprinkle with the seasoned salt, thyme, parsley and pepper. Cover and cook on low for 5 to 5½ hours or until turkey is tender.

Authentic Tandoori Chicken

Serve: 6

Prep time: 5 minutes

Cook time: 4 hours

INGREDIENTS:

1 (1.5-2 kg) chicken, cut into 8 pieces and skin removed

375 g plain yoghurt

10 ml fresh lemon juice

2 cloves garlic, minced

1 tsp. ground coriander

½ tsp. ground cumin

½ tsp. ground cardamom

½ tsp. turmeric

1 tsp. sweet paprika

1 tsp. freshly grated ginger

DIRECTIONS:

1. Combine the yoghurt, lemon juice, coriander, cumin, cardamom, turmeric, paprika, garlic, and ginger in a 4-L zipper-top plastic bag.
2. Add the chicken in the bag and marinate for at least 8 hours and up to 24 hours. Put the chicken and the marinade in the insert of a slow cooker.
3. Cover and cook on high for 4 hours, until the chicken is cooked through. Remove the chicken from the pot and serve warm or at room temperature.

Braised Apple Balsamic Chicken

Prep time: 15 minutes
Cook time: 4 to 5 hours

INGREDIENTS:
30 g butter
15 g plain flour
4 bone-in chicken thighs (about 700 g), skin removed
120 ml chicken broth
60 ml apple cider or juice
60 ml balsamic vinegar
30 ml lemon juice
½ tsp. salt
½ tsp. garlic powder
½ tsp. dried thyme
½ tsp. paprika
½ tsp. pepper

DIRECTIONS:
1. Place chicken in a slow cooker. In a small bowl, combine the broth, cider, vinegar, lemon juice and seasonings; pour over meat. Cover and cook on low for 4 to 5 hours or until chicken is tender.
2. Remove chicken; keep warm. Skim fat from cooking liquid. In a small saucepan, melt butter; stir in flour until smooth. Gradually add cooking liquid. Bring to a boil; cook and stir for 2 to 3 minutes or until thickened. Serve with chicken.

Filipino Chicken Adobo

Prep time: 15 minutes
Cook time: 3 to 3½ hours

INGREDIENTS:
30 ml olive oil
1 kg bone-in, skin-on chicken thighs (about 8), trimmed of fat
450 g red or gold waxy potatoes, scrubbed and cut into eights
2 medium-size carrots, sliced
115 g green beans, ends trimmed
175 ml plain rice vinegar
120 ml low-sodium soy sauce
4 cloves garlic, pressed
1 (5- to 7-cm) piece fresh ginger, peeled and grated (optional)
10 g light brown sugar
1 tsp. black peppercorns
2 bay leaves
175 ml water

DIRECTIONS:
1. In a shallow glass baking dish, stir together the vinegar, soy sauce, garlic, ginger (if using), brown sugar, peppercorns, and bay leaves. Add the chicken and turn to coat. Cover and marinate in the refrigerator for at least 1 hour or as long as overnight.
2. Place the potatoes, carrots, and green beans in the slow cooker. Lift the chicken out of the marinade and pat dry with kitchen towels. Heat the oil in a large frying pan over medium-high heat and cook the chicken, skin side down, until it is a golden brown on both sides, about 2 minutes per side. Transfer the chicken thighs to the crock. Pour the marinade and water into the frying pan and bring to a boil. Pour the sauce into the crock.
3. Cover and cook on high for 3 to 3½ hours, or until the juice of the chicken runs clear. Discard the bay leaves. Serve the chicken and vegetables with the sauce.

Chicken with Apple and Chardonnay Gravy

Prep time: 20 minutes

Cook time: 6 to 8 hours

INGREDIENTS:

6 chicken leg quarters
2 large sweet apples, peeled and cut into wedges
1 large sweet onion, chopped
2 celery ribs, chopped
2 large garlic cloves, minced
120 ml chardonnay

1 envelope brown gravy mix
½ tsp. salt
¼ tsp. pepper
1 tsp. each minced fresh oregano, rosemary and thyme
Hot mashed potatoes

DIRECTIONS:

1. Sprinkle chicken with salt and pepper. Place half of the chicken in a slow cooker. In a bowl, combine the apples, onion and celery; spoon half of the mixture over chicken. Repeat layers.
2. In the same bowl, whisk wine, gravy mix, garlic and herbs until blended; pour over top. Cover and cook on low for 6 to 8 hours or until chicken is tender.
3. Remove chicken to a serving platter; keep warm. Cool the apple mixture slightly; skim fat. In a blender, cover and process apple mixture in batches until smooth. Transfer to a saucepan and heat through over medium heat, stirring occasionally. Serve with chicken and mashed potatoes.

Italian Turkey Sausage and Veggies

Serve: 6

Prep time: 20 minutes

Cook time: 5½ to 6½ hours

INGREDIENTS:

570 g sweet or hot Italian turkey sausage links
800 g tinned diced tomatoes, undrained
2 medium potatoes, cut into 2½-cm pieces
4 small courgettes, cut into 2½-cm slices

1 medium onion, cut into wedges
½ tsp. garlic powder
¼ tsp. crushed red pepper flakes
¼ tsp. dried oregano
¼ tsp. dried basil
1 tbsp. dry bread crumbs
90 g shredded chilli cheese or mild cheddar

DIRECTIONS:

1. In a non-stick frying pan, brown sausages over medium heat. Place in a slow cooker. Add vegetables and seasonings. Cover and cook on low for 5½ to 6½ hours or until a thermometer reads 75°C.
2. Remove sausages and cut into 2½-cm pieces; return to slow cooker. Stir in bread crumbs. Serve in bowls; sprinkle with cheese.

Thai Sesame Chicken Thighs

Serve: 8

Prep time: 20 minutes

Cook time: 5 to 6 hours

INGREDIENTS:

8 bone-in chicken thighs (about 1.4 kg), skin removed
120 ml salsa
120 g creamy peanut butter
30 ml lemon juice
30 ml reduced-sodium soy sauce
1 garlic clove, minced

2 spring onions, sliced
2 tbsps. sesame seeds, toasted
2 tsps. Thai chilli sauce
1 tbsp. chopped deseeded jalapeño pepper
1 tsp. minced fresh ginger
Hot cooked basmati rice (optional)

DIRECTIONS:

1. Place chicken in a slow cooker. In a small bowl, combine the salsa, peanut butter, lemon juice, soy sauce, jalapeño, Thai chilli sauce, garlic and ginger; pour over chicken.
2. Cover and cook on low for 5 to 6 hours or until chicken is tender. Sprinkle with spring onions and sesame seeds. Serve with rice if desired.

CHAPTER 8
SOUP AND STEWS

Creamy Mushroom and Bacon Soup

Serve: 8

Prep time: 10 minutes

Cook time: 3 hours

INGREDIENTS:

450 g chestnut mushrooms, sliced

450 g shiitake mushrooms, stems removed, and caps sliced

700 ml chicken broth

235 ml double cream

30 g dried cep mushrooms

60 ml soy sauce

8 strips streaky bacon, cut into 1¼-cm dice

1 large onion, finely chopped

1 tsp. dried sage leaves, crushed

15 g snipped fresh chives, for garnish

DIRECTIONS:

1. Sauté the bacon in a large frying pan over medium heat until crisp and remove it from the pan to drain.
2. Add the onion and sage to the pan and sauté until the onion is softened. Add the chestnut and shiitake mushrooms and toss until the mixture is combined.
3. Transfer the contents of the frying pan to the insert of a slow cooker. Add the cep mushrooms, soy sauce, broth, and bacon.
4. Cover and cook on high for 3 hours or on low for 5 to 6 hours. At the end of the cooking time, add the cream and stir to combine.
5. Serve the soup garnished with the chives.

Italian Beef Minestrone

Serve: 12

Prep time: 15 minutes

Cook time: 6 hours

INGREDIENTS:

450 g extra-lean beef mince

1 large onion, chopped

285 g frozen corn

800 g tinned tomatoes

400 g tinned cannellini beans, drained

2 ribs celery, sliced

2 small courgette, sliced

100 g macaroni, uncooked

585 ml hot water

2 beef stock cubes

1 clove garlic, minced

½ tsp. salt

2 tsps. Italian seasoning

DIRECTIONS:

1. Brown beef mince in non-stick frying pan.
2. Combine browned beef mince, onion, garlic, tomatoes, cannellini beans, corn, celery, courgette, and macaroni in a slow cooker.
3. Dissolve stock cubes in hot water. Combine with salt and Italian seasoning. Add to a slow cooker.
4. Cover. Cook on low 6 hours.

Nutmeg Carrot Soup

Serve: 8

Prep time: 15 minutes

Cook time: 6 to 8 hours

INGREDIENTS:

60 ml olive oil

2 medium-size brown onions, chopped

2 large rooster potatoes, peeled and chopped

1.4 kg carrots (about 15 medium-size), scrubbed, tops cut off, and chopped

1 or 2 small cloves garlic, pressed

½ tsp. each dried thyme and marjoram

1 to 1.5 L water or chicken broth, plus more as needed

40 g honey

½ to 1 tsp. freshly grated nutmeg, to your taste

Sea salt and freshly ground black pepper, to taste

DIRECTIONS:

1. Heat the oil in a large frying pan over medium heat. Add the onions and cook until softened, 6 to 8 minutes, stirring often to cook evenly.
2. Put the potatoes, carrots, garlic, and herbs in the slow cooker; add the onions and oil, scraping them out of the pan. Add enough of the water to cover everything. Cover and cook on high for 1 hour.
3. Turn the cooker to low and cook until the vegetables are soft, 5 to 7 hours. Purée in batches in a food processor or right in the slow cooker with a handheld immersion blender; the soup will be nice and thick. Stir in the honey and grate the nutmeg right over the crock. Season with salt and pepper. Keep warm on low without letting it come to a boil until serving. Ladle the hot soup into bowls and enjoy.

Black Bean and Tomato Soup

Serve: 4 to 6

Prep time: 10 minutes

Cook time: 5 to 7 hours

INGREDIENTS:

850 g tinned black beans, rinsed and drained

400 g tomatoes with green chillis

400 g diced tomatoes, with their juice

315 g tinned whole kernel corn, drained

250 g tinned chopped roasted green chillis

4 spring onions (white part and 5 cm of the green), sliced

2 cloves garlic, pressed

1 to 1½ tbsps. chilli powder, to your taste

1 tsp. ground cumin

For Serving:

Shredded Cheddar cheese

Soured cream

DIRECTIONS:

1. Put all the ingredients in the slow cooker and stir to combine. Cover and cook on low for 5 to 7 hours.
2. Add some boiling water to thin, if desired. Ladle into individual bowls and serve hot with a sprinkling of shredded cheddar cheese and a dollop of soured cream.

Hearty Italian Vegetable Soup

Prep time: 15 minutes

Cook time: 7½ to 8½ hours

INGREDIENTS:

45 ml olive oil

1 medium-size brown onion, chopped

2 small carrots, diced

2 ribs celery, chopped

2 small courgette, ends trimmed and cubed

400 g tinned red cannellini beans, rinsed, drained, and half the beans mashed

15 g packed fresh flat-leaf parsley leaves, chopped

800 g tinned whole tomatoes, mashed, with their juice

585 ml chicken broth

5 leaves Swiss chard, chopped, or ½ small head Chinese cabbage, cored and chopped

285 g frozen broad beans

115 ml dry red wine

35 g elbow macaroni or little shells

1 tsp. salt

1 bay leaf

Freshly ground black pepper, to taste

Freshly grated Parmesan cheese, for serving

DIRECTIONS:

1. In a large frying pan, heat the olive oil over medium heat. Add the onion, carrots, celery, and courgette and cook, stirring often, until just softened, about 5 minutes. Transfer to the slow cooker and add the cannellini beans, salt, bay leaf, pepper, parsley, tomatoes and their juice, broad beans, and broth. Add water to come about 2½ cm above the vegetables. Cover and cook on low for 5 hours.
2. Add the Swiss chard and wine, cover, and continue to cook on low for another 2 to 3 hours. Remove the bay leaf.
3. Stir in the pasta, cover, and cook on high until the pasta is just tender, about 30 minutes. Ladle into soup bowls and serve hot with lots of Parmesan.

Lemony Red Lentil Soup

Prep time: 10 minutes

Cook time: 6 to 7 hours

INGREDIENTS:

30 ml olive oil

1 medium-size brown onion, finely chopped

2 ribs celery, chopped

450 g dried red lentils, picked over and rinsed

1 tsp. ground cumin

1 tsp. ground turmeric

¾ tsp. ground coriander

30 ml fresh lemon juice

1.5 L chicken or vegetable broth

Salt and freshly ground black pepper, to taste (optional)

DIRECTIONS:

1. In a large frying pan, heat the olive oil over medium heat. Add the onion and celery and cook, stirring often, until just softened, about 5 minutes. Transfer to the slow cooker, along with the lentils, spices, and lemon juice. Add the broth and enough water to come about 7 cm above the vegetables. Cover and cook on high for 1 hour.
2. Turn the cooker to low and cook the soup for 5 to 6 hours. Season with salt and pepper, if desired. Add water to thin if the soup is too thick. Ladle into bowls and serve hot.

Green Split Pea Soup

Prep time: 10 minutes

Cook time: 12 to 15 hours

INGREDIENTS:
225 g dried green split peas
1.2 L water
80 g chopped shallots
75 g chopped celery
75 g chopped carrots
1 bay leaf
½ tsp. dried thyme or 1½ tsps. chopped fresh thyme
¼ tsp. dried sage or 1 tsp. chopped fresh sage (optional)
Salt, to taste
Dash of cayenne pepper
Warm bread or croutons, for serving

DIRECTIONS:
1. Put the split peas in a colander and rinse under cold running water. Pick over, discarding any that are discoloured. Put in the slow cooker along with the water, shallots, carrots, celery, bay leaf, thyme, and sage, if using. Stir to combine. Cover and cook on low until the peas are completely tender, 12 to 15 hours. Remove the bay leaf.
2. Purée the soup, using a blender, food processor, immersion blender, or the fine blade of a food mill. You may need to do this in batches. Season the soup with salt (start with about ¼ teaspoon) and a just a bit of cayenne pepper. Serve hot with warm bread or croutons.

Creamy Courgette Soup

Prep time: 10 minutes

Cook time: 6 to 7 hours

INGREDIENTS:
90 g unsalted butter, cut into 3 or 4 pieces
680 g courgette, ends trimmed, and cut into chunks
1 large brown onion, chopped
700 ml chicken or vegetable broth
Salt and freshly ground black pepper, to taste
235 ml single cream
½ tsp. curry powder
25 g white basmati rice or long-grain white rice
1 tbsp. chopped fresh basil
Croutons, for serving (optional)

DIRECTIONS:
1. Put the butter, onion, curry powder, and courgette in the slow cooker, cover, and cook on high to sweat the vegetables for 30 minutes.
2. Add the rice, basil, and broth, cover, and cook on low for 5 to 6 hours.
3. Purée with a handheld immersion blender or transfer to a food processor or blender and purée in batches. Season with salt and pepper. Stir in the single cream, cover, and continue to cook on low until heated through, 20 minutes; do not boil.
4. Ladle the hot soup into bowls and garnish with croutons, if desired.

Beef Barley Soup

Prep time: 10 minutes
Cook time: 5 to 7 hours

INGREDIENTS:
450 g lean stewing meat, cut into bite-sized pieces
1 L beef broth
830 g tinned tomatoes
340 g low-sodium tomato or V8 juice
100 g pearl barley, uncooked
235 ml water
70 g corn, fresh or frozen
75 g onions, chopped
35 g cut green beans, fresh or frozen

DIRECTIONS:
1. Combine all ingredients in a slow cooker.
2. Cover. Cook on high 5 to 7 hours, until vegetables are cooked to your liking.

Black-Eyed Bean and Beef Soup

Serve: 6

Prep time: 25 minutes
Cook time: 8 to 10 hours

INGREDIENTS:
450 g dried black-eyed beans
2 tins lentil and bacon soup
500 to 750 ml water
4 large carrots, peeled and sliced
1.4 kg beef chuck roast, cut into 5-cm cubes
½ tsp. salt
½ tsp. pepper

DIRECTIONS:
1. Rinse and drain the beans.
2. Combine all ingredients in a slow cooker.
3. Cook on low 8 to 10 hours, or until beans and beef are tender.

Beef Macaroni Soup

Serve: 6

Prep time: 10 minutes
Cook time: 6¼ to 8¼ hours

INGREDIENTS:

450 g extra-lean beef mince	230 g tomato passata
¼ tsp. black pepper	15 ml low-sodium soy sauce
¼ tsp. dried oregano	75 g carrots, sliced
¼ tsp. seasoned salt	75 g celery, sliced
1 envelope dry onion soup mix	100 g macaroni, cooked
700 ml hot water	30 g grated parmesan cheese

DIRECTIONS:
1. Combine all ingredients except macaroni and parmesan cheese in a slow cooker.
2. Cook on low 6 to 8 hours.
3. Turn to high. Add macaroni and Parmesan cheese.
4. Cook for another 15 to 20 minutes.

Creamy Artichoke and Leek Soup

Serve: 6

Prep time: 10 minutes

Cook time: 6 to 7 hours

INGREDIENTS:

90 g unsalted butter, cut into 4 or 5 pieces
3 leeks (white part and 2-cm of the green), washed well and thinly sliced
850 g frozen artichoke hearts, thawed

1 small white onion, chopped
1.5 L chicken broth
235 ml double cream
Salt and white pepper, to taste
Croutons, for serving (optional)

DIRECTIONS:

1. Place the butter, onion, and leeks in the slow cooker. Turn to high, cover, and sweat the vegetables for 30 minutes.
2. Add the artichoke hearts and broth, cover, and cook on low for 5 to 6 hours.
3. Purée with a handheld immersion blender or transfer to a food processor or blender and purée in batches. Strain the soup by pushing it with a spatula through a large-mesh strainer to remove any fibres. Season with salt and pepper. Return the soup to the cooker, stir in the cream, cover, and cook on low until heated through, about 20 minutes; do not boil.
4. Ladle the hot soup into bowls and garnish with croutons, if desired.

Beef and Lentil Soup

Serve: 10

Prep time: 20 minutes

Cook time: 8 hours

INGREDIENTS:

450 g extra-lean beef mince
830 g crushed tomatoes, undrained
200 g dry lentils, rinsed
1 medium onion, chopped
280 g cubed potatoes
75 g chopped celery

75 g diced carrots
85 g medium-sized pearl barley
1.9 L water
2 tsps. beef stock granules
½ tsp. salt
½ tsp. lemon pepper seasoning

DIRECTIONS:

1. Brown beef mince with onions in a frying pan. Drain.
2. Combine all ingredients except tomatoes in a slow cooker.
3. Cook on low 6 hours, or until tender.
4. Add tomatoes. Cook on low 2 more hours.

Onion Soup

Serve: 4

Prep time: 10 minutes

Cook time: 6 to 7 hours

INGREDIENTS:

4 heads garlic
1 large brown onion, chopped
1.2 L chicken broth

170 g tomato puree
45 ml extra-virgin olive oil
Hot fresh crusty bread, for serving

DIRECTIONS:

1. Fill a small deep saucepan with water and bring to a boil. Separate the garlic heads into cloves and toss them into the boiling water; blanch for 1 minute exactly. Drain the garlic cloves in a colander and rinse under cold running water; peel with a paring knife.
2. Combine the garlic cloves, onion, broth, and tomato puree in the slow cooker and stir to blend. Cover and cook on low for 6 to 7 hours.
3. Purée the soup with a handheld immersion blender or transfer to a food processor or blender and purée in batches. Before serving, add the olive oil. Ladle into soup bowls and serve hot with fresh crusty bread. You can drizzle the top of the soup with a bit more olive oil if you like.

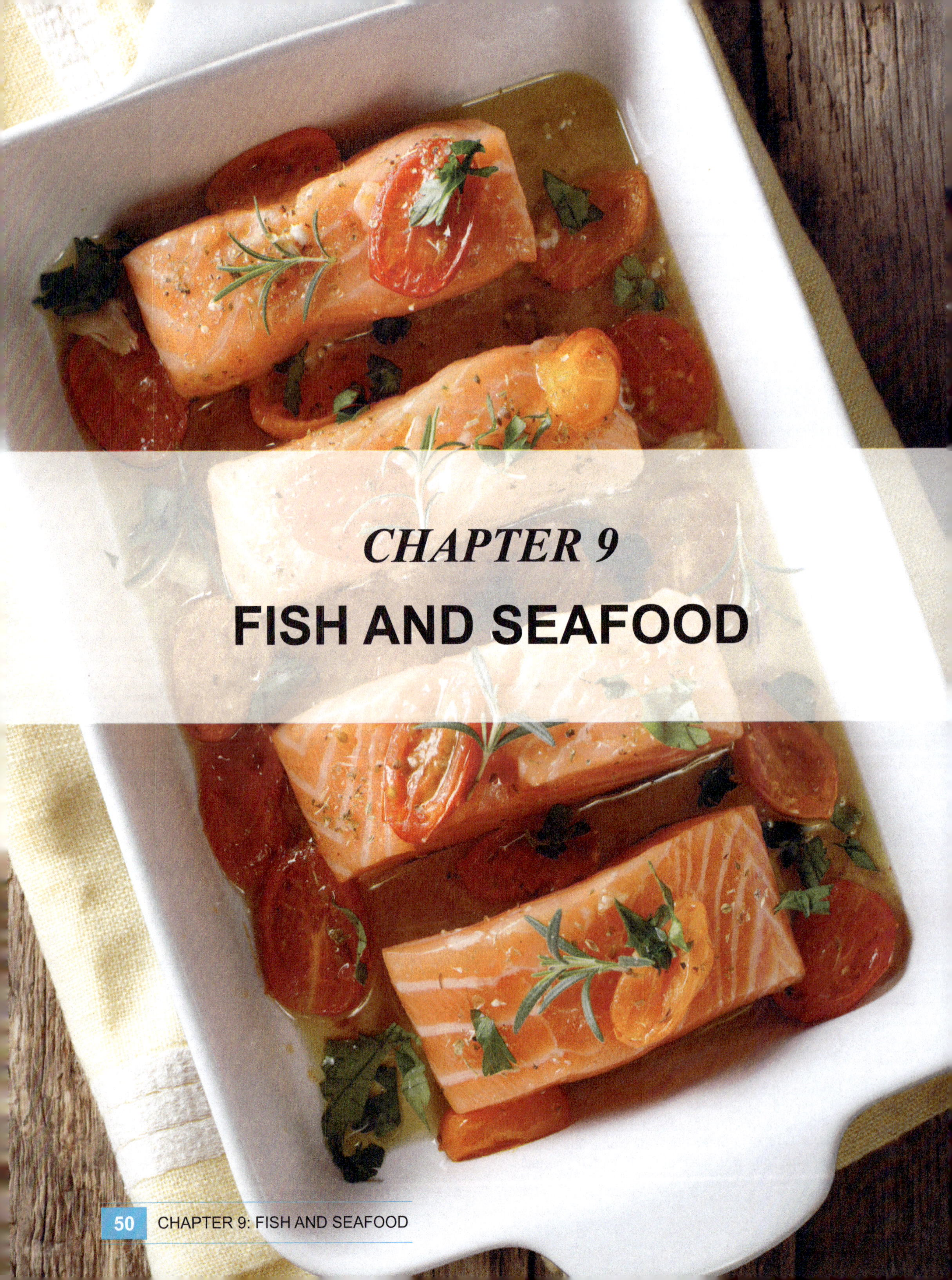

CHAPTER 9
FISH AND SEAFOOD

Wine-Glazed Salmon with Lemon

Serve: 4

Prep time: 10 minutes
Cook time: 1½ hours

INGREDIENTS:
4 salmon fillets (3 cm thick and 170 g each)
475 ml water
235 ml white wine
1 medium carrot, sliced
1 medium onion, sliced
1 celery rib, sliced
30 ml lemon juice
3 fresh thyme sprigs
1 fresh rosemary sprig
1 bay leaf
½ tsp. salt
¼ tsp. pepper
Lemon wedges

DIRECTIONS:
1. In a slow cooker, combine the first 11 ingredients. Cook, covered, on low 45 minutes.
2. Carefully place fillets in liquid; add additional warm water to cover if needed. Cook, covered, 45 to 55 minutes or just until fish flakes easily with a fork. A thermometer inserted in fish should read at least 65°C. Remove fish from cooking liquid. Serve warm or cold with lemon wedges.

Ritzy Seafood Mcdley

Serve: 10 to 12

Prep time: 20 minutes
Cook time: 3 to 4 hours

INGREDIENTS:
450 g prawns, peeled and deveined
450 g crab meat
450 g small scallops
600 g tinned cream of celery soup
600 ml milk
30 g butter, melted
1 tsp. Old Bay seasoning
¼ to ½ tsp. salt
¼ tsp. pepper

DIRECTIONS:
1. Layer prawns, crab, and scallops in a slow cooker.
2. Combine soup and milk. Pour over seafood.
3. Mix together butter and spices and pour over top.
4. Cover. Cook on low 3 to 4 hours.
5. Serve over rice or noodles.

Curried Prawn

Prep time: 5 minutes
Cook time: 2 to 3 hours

INGREDIENTS:
300 g tinned cream of mushroom soup
250 g cooked prawns
245 g soured cream
1 small onion, chopped
1 tsp. curry powder

DIRECTIONS:
1. Combine all ingredients except soured cream in a slow cooker.
2. Cover. Cook on low 2 to 3 hours.
3. Ten minutes before serving, stir in soured cream.
4. Serve over rice or puff pastry.

Classic Prawn Jambalaya

Prep time: 20 minutes
Cook time: 2¼ hours

INGREDIENTS:
30 g butter
450 g medium-sized prawns, shelled and deveined
800 g tinned chopped tomatoes
2 medium onions, chopped
2 green peppers, chopped
3 ribs celery, chopped
120 g cooked lean ham
2 garlic cloves, chopped
275 g quick cooking rice, uncooked
350 ml fat-free low sodium beef broth
2 tbsps. fresh chopped parsley
1 tsp. dried basil
½ tsp. dried thyme
¼ tsp. black pepper
⅛ tsp. cayenne pepper
1 tbsp. chopped parsley, for garnish

DIRECTIONS:
1. One-half hour before assembling recipe, melt butter in a slow cooker set on high. Add onions, peppers, celery, ham, and garlic. Cook for 30 minutes.
2. Add rice. Cover and cook for 15 minutes.
3. Add broth, tomatoes, 2 tbsps. parsley, and remaining seasonings. Cover and cook on high for 1 hour.
4. Add prawns and cook on high for 30 minutes, or until liquid is absorbed.
5. Garnish with 1 tbsp. parsley.

Citrus Sea Bass

Prep time: 15 minutes
Cook time: 1½ hours

INGREDIENTS:
15 ml olive oil or toasted sesame oil
675 g sea bass fillets, rinsed and blotted dry
1 medium-size white onion, chopped
10 g minced fresh flat-leaf parsley
1 tbsp. grated lemon, lime, or orange zest or a combination
45 ml dry white wine or water
Sea salt and white pepper, to taste
For Serving:
Lemon wedges
Lime wedges
Cold tartar sauce

DIRECTIONS:
1. Coat the slow cooker with rapeseed oil spray or butter and arrange the fish in the crock. Season lightly with salt and white pepper, then add the onion, parsley, and zest. Drizzle with the wine and oil. Cover and cook on high for 1½ hours.
2. Carefully lift the fish out of the cooker with a plastic spatula or pancake turner. Serve immediately with lemon and lime wedges and tartar sauce.

Wine Braised Trout with Parsley

Prep time: 10 minutes
Cook time: ¾ to 1¼ hours

INGREDIENTS:
6 boned trout (680 g), head and tail left on
Salt and freshly ground black pepper, to taste
30 g unsalted butter
2 medium-size shallots, chopped
10 g chopped fresh flat-leaf parsley
1 lemon, sliced
350 g dry white wine

DIRECTIONS:
1. Coat the slow cooker with rapeseed oil spray. Sprinkle the inside and outside of the fish with salt and pepper and arrange the trout in the cooker; they can be lying against each other.
2. In a small frying pan over medium heat, melt the butter, then cook the shallots until softened, 3 to 4 minutes; stir in the parsley and stuff some of the mixture inside each trout. Arrange the lemon slices on top.
3. Heat the wine in a saucepan or the microwave until boiling. Pour around the trout. Cover and cook on high until the fish is tender, 45 minutes to 1¼ hours.

Green Chilli and Prawn Tacos

Prep time: 25 minutes

Cook time: 6 to 7 hours

INGREDIENTS:
4 poblano chillis, stemmed, deseeded, and cut into 1-cm-wide strips
3 onions, halved and thinly sliced
45 ml extra-virgin olive oil
4 garlic cloves, thinly sliced
½ tsp. dried oregano
Salt and pepper, to taste
700 g extra-large prawns, peeled, deveined, tails removed, and cut into 2½-cm pieces
2 tbsps. minced fresh coriander
1 tsp. grated lime zest plus 1 tsp. juice
12 to 18 corn tortillas, warmed

DIRECTIONS:
1. Toss poblanos and onions with 60 ml oil, garlic, oregano, ½ tsp. salt, and ½ tsp. pepper in slow cooker. Cover and cook until vegetables are tender, 6 to 7 hours on low or 4 to 5 hours on high.
2. Season prawns with salt and pepper and stir into a slow cooker. Cover and cook on high until prawn pieces are opaque throughout, 30 to 40 minutes. Strain prawn mixture, discarding cooking liquid, and return to now-empty slow cooker. Stir in coriander, lime zest and juice, and remaining 15 ml oil. Season with salt and pepper to taste. Serve with tortillas.

Hearty Cod Stew

Prep time: 30 minutes

Cook time: 6½ to 8½ hours

INGREDIENTS:
450 g potatoes (about 2 medium), peeled and finely chopped
450 g cod fillets, cut into 2½-cm pieces
400 g tinned diced tomatoes, undrained
350 ml vegetable or chicken broth
300 g tinned condensed cream of celery soup, undiluted
120 ml white wine or additional vegetable broth
340 g fat-free evaporated milk
300 g frozen corn, thawed
400 g tinned broad beans, thawed
1 large onion, finely chopped
1 celery rib, finely chopped
1 medium carrot, finely chopped
4 garlic cloves, minced
1 bay leaf
1 tsp. lemon-pepper seasoning
1 tsp. dried parsley flakes
1 tsp. dried rosemary, crushed
½ tsp. salt

DIRECTIONS:
1. In a slow cooker, combine the first 15 ingredients. Cook, covered, on low 6-8 hours or until potatoes are tender.
2. Remove bay leaf. Stir in cod, tomatoes and milk; cook, covered, 30-35 minutes longer or until fish just begins to flake easily with a fork.

Braised Scallops with Leeks

Serve: 4

Prep time: 20 minutes

Cook time: 3 to 4 hours

INGREDIENTS:

1 tsp. extra-virgin olive oil
450 g leeks, white and light green parts only, halved lengthwise, thinly sliced, and washed thoroughly
700 g large sea scallops, tendons removed

30 g grated Pecorino Romano cheese
4 garlic cloves, minced
80 ml double cream
60 ml dry white wine
Salt and pepper, to taste
2 tbsps. minced fresh parsley

DIRECTIONS:

1. Microwave leeks, garlic, and oil in bowl, stirring occasionally, until leeks are softened, about 5 minutes; transfer to a slow cooker. Stir in cream and wine. Cover and cook until leeks are tender but not mushy, 3 to 4 hours on low or 2 to 3 hours on high.
2. Season scallops with salt and pepper and nestle into a slow cooker. Spoon portion of sauce over scallops. Cover and cook on high until sides of scallops are firm and centres are opaque, 30 to 40 minutes.
3. Transfer scallops to serving dish. Stir Pecorino into sauce and season with salt and pepper to taste. Spoon sauce over scallops and sprinkle with parsley. Serve.

Thai Green Curry Prawns and Sweet Potato.

Serve: 4 to 6

Prep time: 25 minutes

Cook time: 4½ to 5½ hours

INGREDIENTS:

15 ml rapeseed oil
700 g large prawns, peeled, deveined, and tails removed
230 g mangetout, strings removed and cut into 2½-cm pieces
470 ml chicken broth, plus extra as needed
30 ml Thai green curry paste

15 g instant tapioca
900 g sweet potatoes, peeled and cut into 2½-cm pieces
385 ml tinned coconut milk
Salt and pepper, to taste
15 g fresh coriander leaves
30 ml lime juice
15 ml fish sauce

DIRECTIONS:

1. Whisk broth, curry paste, and tapioca together in a slow cooker, then stir in potatoes. Cover and cook until flavours meld and potatoes are tender, 4 to 5 hours on low or 3 to 4 hours on high.
2. Microwave coconut milk in bowl until hot, about 2 minutes. Season prawns with salt and pepper. Stir prawns, coconut milk, lime juice, and fish sauce into curry. Cover and cook on high until prawns are opaque throughout, about 30 minutes.
3. Microwave mangetout and oil in bowl, stirring occasionally, until mangetout are tender, 3 to 5 minutes. Stir mangetout into curry. Adjust consistency with extra hot broth as needed. Stir in coriander and season with salt and pepper to taste. Serve.

Smoky Salmon Fettuccine

Serve: 4

Prep time: 10 minutes

Cook time: 1 to 2 hours

INGREDIENTS:

470 ml double cream
85 to 115 g smoked salmon, chopped or flaked into 1¼-cm pieces
450 g fresh fettuccine, regular egg or spinach flavoured
30 ml olive oil (optional)
Freshly ground black pepper, to taste

DIRECTIONS:

1. Combine the cream and the smoked salmon in the slow cooker. Cover and cook on low until very hot, 1 to 2 hours.
2. Meanwhile, cook the fettuccine in boiling water until tender to the bite, about 3 minutes. Take care not to overcook. Toss with the olive oil if the pasta is to stand for over 5 minutes. Add the fettuccine to the hot sauce and toss to coat evenly. If your cooker is large enough, just add the pasta to the cooker; if not, pour the sauce over the pasta in a shallow, heated bowl. Garnish with a few grinds of black pepper and serve immediately.

Miso Poached Salmon

Prep time: 5 minutes

Cook time: 1½ hours

INGREDIENTS:

1.5 kg salmon fillets	sherry
45 g white Miso	60 g honey
60 ml rice wine (mirin) or dry	2 tsps. freshly grated ginger

DIRECTIONS:

1. Place the salmon in the insert of a slow cooker.
2. Combine the miso, honey, rice wine, and ginger in a mixing bowl and stir.
3. Pour the sauce over the salmon in the slow cooker. Cover and cook on high for 1½ hours, until the salmon is cooked through and registers 75°C on an instant-read thermometer inserted in the centre of a thick fillet.
4. Carefully remove the salmon from the slow-cooker insert with a large spatula. Remove the skin from the underside of the salmon (if necessary) and arrange the salmon on a serving platter.
5. Strain the sauce through a fine-mesh sieve into a saucepan. Boil the sauce, reduce it to a syrupy consistency, and serve with the salmon.

Cheddar Tuna-Stuffed Potatoes

Prep time: 10 minutes

Cook time: 3¾ to 6 hours

INGREDIENTS:

4 medium-size rooster potatoes, scrubbed	drained
175 g finely shredded Cheddar cheese	120 g soured cream
	60 ml milk
170 g tinned water-packed tuna,	1 spring onion (white and some of the green), thinly sliced

DIRECTIONS:

1. Prick each dripping-wet potato with a fork or the tip of a sharp knife and pile them into the slow cooker; do not add water. Cover and cook until fork-tender, on high for 3 to 5 hours or on low for 6 to 8 hours.
2. Remove the potatoes from the cooker with tongs and cut in half lengthwise. Scoop out the centre of each half with a large spoon, leaving enough potato to keep the shell intact. Put the potato flesh in a bowl and add two-thirds of the cheese, the milk, tuna, soured cream, and spring onion. Mash the filling with a fork and spoon it back into the shells, mounding it high. Return to the slow cooker, setting down the stuffed potatoes in a single layer if possible so that they touch each other. Sprinkle with the remaining cheese. Cover and cook on high for 45 minutes to 1 hour. Remove carefully from the cooker and serve immediately.

Slow Cooker Poached Salmon Steaks

Prep time: 10 minutes

Cook time: 1½ hours

INGREDIENTS:

4 (225 g) salmon steaks or fillets, rinsed and blotted dry	1 sprig fresh dill
235 ml chicken broth or water	1 thick slice onion
120 ml dry white wine	3 sprigs fresh flat-leaf parsley
Sea salt, to taste	For Serving:
2 black peppercorns	Lemon wedges
	Cold tartar sauce

DIRECTIONS:

1. Coat the slow cooker with rapeseed oil spray and arrange the salmon in it. The steaks can be set tightly side by side; tuck the ends of fillets under themselves to even out the thickness of the fish so it can cook evenly.
2. Heat the broth and wine in a saucepan or the microwave until boiling. Pour around the salmon. Sprinkle the steaks with some salt, then add the peppercorns, dill, onion slice, and parsley to the liquid around the steaks. Cover and cook on high until the salmon is opaque and firm to the touch, about 1½ hours.
3. Carefully lift the salmon out of the cooker with a rubber spatula or pancake turner. Serve immediately while still hot or cool until lukewarm in the poaching liquid and refrigerate until cold. Accompany with lemon wedges and tartar sauce.

CHAPTER 10
VEGETABLES

Roasted Cauliflower with Tomato Cashew Sauce

Serve: 6

Prep time: 15 minutes

Cook time: 4 to 5 hours

INGREDIENTS:

30 g ghee or rapeseed oil

2 tomatoes, roughly chopped

1 fresh green chilli, chopped

45 g raw cashews, soaked in water for 2 hours and drained

1 large head cauliflower, outer leaves trimmed

1 red onion, sliced

2½-cm piece fresh ginger, cut into strips

4 garlic cloves, sliced

155 ml hot water

1 tsp. cumin seeds

1 tsp. coriander seeds

1 tsp. salt

1 tsp. Kashmiri chilli powder

1 tsp. turmeric

1 tsp. garam masala

1 tbsp. dried fenugreek leaves

Handful fresh coriander leaves, chopped

DIRECTIONS:

1. Preheat the slow cooker on high for 15 minutes, or use the sauté setting if you have one. Add the onions, ginger, garlic, tomatoes, and green chilli. Stir and cook for 10 minutes.
2. Add the drained cashews and place the head of cauliflower on top of everything.
3. Heat the ghee or rapeseed oil, if using, in a frying pan and toast the cumin and coriander seeds until they are fragrant. Pour them over the cauliflower head and sprinkle in the salt, chilli powder, turmeric, and garam masala.
4. Add the water. Cover and cook on low for 4 to 5 hours, or on high for 2 to 3 hours.
5. When it's cooked (you can check by sticking a sharp knife through the middle), transfer the cauliflower head to a shallow oven-proof dish. Using an immersion or regular blender, blend the cooking liquid that's left in the slow cooker to make a smooth sauce. It should be like a thick batter; if it's too thick, you can add a little hot water.
6. Check and adjust the salt, if required. Add the dried fenugreek leaves and then pour the sauce over the cauliflower head. Place in the oven at 205°C for 5 to 10 minutes to crisp up.
7. Sprinkle on some fresh coriander leaves and serve in chunky wedges.

Summer Squash and Kale Stew

Serve: 2

Prep time: 10 minutes

Cook time: 4 hours

INGREDIENTS:

400 g tinned plum tomatoes, roughly chopped

450 ml low-sodium vegetable broth

150 g tinned chickpeas, drained and rinsed

100 g quinoa

75 g diced summer squash

120 g fresh kale

1 tbsp. Italian herb blend

⅛ tsp. sea salt

DIRECTIONS:

1. Put all the ingredients into the slow cooker, stirring to mix them together thoroughly.
2. Cover and cook on low for 4 hours.

Indian Spiced Potatoes and Cauliflower

Serve: 6

Prep time: 15 minutes

Cook time: 3 hours

INGREDIENTS:

1 large cauliflower, cored and cut into florets
30 ml mustard oil
2 tsps. mustard seeds
2 tsps. cumin seeds
1 onion, finely chopped
3 garlic cloves, finely chopped
2 red potatoes, peeled and cut into 4-cm cubes
200 g tinned tomatoes
1 tbsp. freshly grated ginger
1 tsp. salt
1 tsp. turmeric
1 tsp. chilli powder
1 or 2 fresh green chillis, finely chopped
1 tsp. dried fenugreek leaves
1 tsp. garam masala
Handful fresh coriander leaves, chopped

DIRECTIONS:

1. Prepare your cauliflower and make sure it's thoroughly dry before cooking.
2. Heat the oil in a frying pan (or in the slow cooker if you have a sear setting). Add the mustard seeds, and as they sizzle, add the cumin seeds.
3. Add the onions and garlic, and cook for 1 minute before adding the potatoes and cauliflower to the slow cooker along with the tomatoes, ginger, salt, turmeric, chilli powder, chopped chillis, and dried fenugreek leaves.
4. Turn the cooker to low and cook for 3 hours, or for 2 hours on high. Give the dish a stir in the first hour, and it will release enough liquid to cook.
5. Before serving, sprinkle with garam masala and fresh coriander leaves.

Tomato Stuffed Spiced Aubergines

Serve: 4

Prep time: 15 minutes

Cook time: 5 to 6 hours

INGREDIENTS:

30 ml extra-virgin olive oil
550 g Italian aubergines, halved lengthwise
400 g tinned diced tomatoes, drained
60 g Pecorino Romano cheese, grated
1 onion, finely chopped
3 garlic cloves, minced
2 tsps. minced fresh oregano or ½ tsp. dried
¼ tsp. ground cinnamon
Salt and pepper, to taste
⅛ tsp. cayenne pepper
35 g pine nuts, toasted
15 ml red wine vinegar
2 tbsps. minced fresh parsley

DIRECTIONS:

1. Microwave onion, 15 ml oil, garlic, oregano, cinnamon, ¼ tsp. salt, and cayenne in bowl, stirring occasionally, until onion is softened, about 5 minutes; transfer to a slow cooker. Stir in tomatoes, ¾ of the Pecorino, pine nuts, and vinegar. Season aubergine halves with salt and pepper and nestle cut side down into slow cooker (aubergines may overlap slightly). Cover and cook until aubergines are tender, 5 to 6 hours on low or 3 to 4 hours on high.
2. Transfer aubergine halves cut side up to serving dish. Using 2 forks, gently push aubergine flesh to sides of each half to make room for filling. Stir remaining oil into tomato mixture and season with salt and pepper to taste. Mound tomato mixture evenly into aubergines and sprinkle with parsley and remaining Pecorino. Serve.

Spicy Potato Stuffed Peppers

Prep time: 15 minutes

Cook time: 4 hours

INGREDIENTS:

5 ml rapeseed oil
4 medium waxy potatoes
2 green peppers
2 red peppers
140 g frozen peas
1 tbsp. fenugreek leaves
2½-cm piece fresh ginger, grated

1 tbsp. finely chopped fresh coriander leaves
1 tsp. cumin seeds
1 tsp. salt
1 fresh green chilli, finely chopped
1 tsp. garam masala

DIRECTIONS:

1. Boil the potatoes with the skin on until they're soft (about 15 minutes), then leave to cool. (I always boil potatoes with the skin on, as it stops them taking on too much water and becoming mushy.) Peel off their skins and dice the potatoes.
2. Preheat the slow cooker on high and make sure the 4 peppers will fit into the cooker side by side.
3. Heat the oil in a small frying pan, and then toast the cumin seeds until fragrant, about 1 minute. Add the peas to soften.
4. Put the toasted cumin and peas in a large bowl. Then add the cooked potatoes with the salt, chilli, garam masala, fenugreek leaves, ginger, and fresh coriander leaves, and mix together. Taste the filling and adjust the seasoning.
5. Slice the tops off the peppers, keeping the stalks intact. Remove the seeds and discard. Divide the potato mixture into 4 portions and stuff each of the peppers.
6. If you have a tray for the inside of your slow cooker, place this inside. If not, crumple up some foil to make a little tray for the peppers to sit on.
7. Place the stuffed peppers on the tray inside the cooker. Replace the top of each of the peppers. Pour about 60 to 80 ml of water into the cooker outside of the tray (so the peppers are not sitting in the water).
8. Cook on low for 4 hours, or for 2 hours on high.

Curried Aubergine and Potato

Prep time: 10 minutes

Cook time: 2 hours

INGREDIENTS:

30 ml mustard oil
2 aubergine, about 450 g total, cut into 2½-cm lengths
2 red potatoes, peeled and cut into 2½-cm lengths
1 onion, finely sliced
200 g tinned tomatoes
2 tsps. mustard seeds

2 tsps. cumin seeds
1 tsp. turmeric
1 fresh green chilli, finely chopped
1 tbsp. freshly grated ginger
1 tsp. sea salt
1 tsp. garam masala
Handful fresh coriander leaves, chopped

DIRECTIONS:

1. Heat the oil in a frying pan (or in the slow cooker if you have a sear setting). Add the mustard seeds, and as they are sizzling add the cumin seeds until they become fragrant.
2. Turn the slow cooker to high and add the spices with the sliced onion, tomatoes, turmeric, chopped chilli, and grated ginger.
3. Stir in the aubergine and potatoes. Cover and cook on high for 2 hours, or for 3 to 4 hours on low.
4. When you are ready to serve, add the salt, garam masala, and fresh coriander leaves.

Tempeh Shepherd's Pie

Serve: 2

Prep time: 10 minutes
Cook time: 8 hours

INGREDIENTS:
350 g prepared mashed potatoes
230 g tempeh
120 g frozen peas, thawed
70 g diced carrots
25 g minced onions
2 tbsps. shredded sharp cheddar cheese
⅛ tsp. sea salt
Freshly ground black pepper, to taste

DIRECTIONS:
1. Put the peas, carrots, onions, and tempeh in the slow cooker and gently stir to combine. Season the mixture with the salt and black pepper.
2. Spread the prepared mashed potatoes over the tempeh and vegetable mixture.
3. Cover and cook on low for 8 hours.
4. Sprinkle with the cheese just before serving.

Spinach and Mushroom Biryani

Serve: 4 to 6

Prep time: 20 minutes
Cook time: 2 to 3 hours

INGREDIENTS:
For the Sauce:
185 g plain yoghurt
2 tbsps. chopped fresh mint
2 tbsps. chopped fresh coriander
1 garlic clove, minced
Salt and pepper, to taste

For the Biryani:
45 ml extra-virgin olive oil
450 g chestnut mushrooms, trimmed and thinly sliced
350 ml vegetable broth
275 g basmati rice, rinsed
170 g baby spinach, coarsely chopped
1 onion, finely chopped
40 g sultanas
15 g sliced almonds, toasted
4 garlic cloves, minced
2 tsps. garam masala
Salt and pepper, to taste
½ tsp. turmeric
⅛ tsp. cayenne pepper
2 tbsps. chopped fresh coriander
2 tbsps. chopped fresh mint

DIRECTIONS:
1. For the sauce: Combine all ingredients in bowl and season with salt and pepper to taste. Refrigerate until ready to serve.
2. For the Biryani: Lightly coat slow cooker with rapeseed oil spray. Microwave onion, oil, garlic, garam masala, 1 tsp. salt, turmeric, and cayenne in bowl, stirring occasionally, until onion is softened, about 5 minutes; transfer to prepared slow cooker.
3. Microwave broth in the bowl until steaming, about 5 minutes. Stir broth and rice into a slow cooker. Spread mushrooms evenly on top of rice mixture. Gently press 16 by 15-cm sheet of greaseproof paper onto surface of mushrooms, folding down edges as needed. Cover and cook until rice is tender and all broth is absorbed, 2 to 3 hours on high.
4. Discard greaseproof. Sprinkle spinach and sultanas on top of rice, cover, and let sit until spinach is wilted, about 5 minutes. Add coriander and mint, and fluff rice with fork until combined. Season with salt and pepper to taste. Sprinkle with almonds and serve, passing sauce separately.

Thai Butternut Squash and Tofu Curry

Prep time: 20 minutes

Cook time: 3 to 4 hours

INGREDIENTS:

1 onion, finely chopped

45 g Thai red curry paste

2 tbsps. grated fresh ginger

4 garlic cloves, minced

20 ml rapeseed oil

900 g butternut squash, peeled, deseeded, and cut into 2½-cm pieces

400 g extra-firm tofu, cut into 2-cm pieces

235 ml vegetable broth, plus extra as needed

2 tsps. instant tapioca

1 red pepper, stemmed, deseeded, and cut into ½-cm-wide strips

235 ml canned coconut milk

15 ml lime juice, plus extra for seasoning

Salt and pepper, to taste

10 g fresh coriander leaves

35 g chopped dry-roasted peanuts

DIRECTIONS:

1. Microwave onion, curry paste, 1 tbsp. ginger, garlic, and 15 ml oil in bowl, stirring occasionally, until onion is softened, about 5 minutes; transfer to a slow cooker. Stir in squash, tofu, broth, and tapioca. Cover and cook until squash is tender, 3 to 4 hours on low or 2 to 3 hours on high.
2. Microwave red pepper with remaining 1 tsp. oil in the bowl, stirring occasionally, until tender, about 5 minutes. Stir red pepper, coconut milk, lime juice, and remaining 1 tbsp. ginger into a slow cooker. Cover and cook on high until heated through, about 10 minutes.
3. Adjust sauce consistency with extra hot broth as needed. Season with salt, pepper, and extra lime juice to taste. Sprinkle individual portions with coriander and peanuts before serving.

Curried Sweet Potatoes and Broccoli

Prep time: 10 minutes

Cook time: 6 to 8 hours

INGREDIENTS:

2 medium sweet potatoes, cut into 2½-cm pieces

235 ml light coconut milk

75 g broccoli florets

35 g toasted cashews

25 g diced onions

1 tsp. minced fresh ginger

1 tsp. minced garlic

Pinch red pepper flakes

1 tbsp. curry powder

1 tsp. garam masala

DIRECTIONS:

1. Put the sweet potatoes, broccoli, and onions into the slow cooker.
2. In a small bowl, whisk together the coconut milk, ginger, garlic, red pepper flakes, curry powder, and garam masala. Pour this mixture over the vegetables.
3. Cover and cook on low for 6 to 8 hours until the vegetables are very tender but not falling apart.
4. Just before serving, add the cashews and stir thoroughly.

CHAPTER 11
STARTER AND DESSERTS

Chilli Chicken Wings

Makes about 4 dozen

Prep time: 15 minutes

Cook time: 6 to 8 hours

INGREDIENTS:

2.3 kg chicken wings (about 25 wings)
350 g chilli sauce
60 ml lemon juice
60 ml black treacle
6 garlic cloves, minced
30 ml Worcestershire sauce
3 drops hot pepper sauce
1 tbsp. chilli powder
1 tbsp. salsa
1 tsp. garlic salt

DIRECTIONS:

1. Cut chicken wings into three sections, discarding wing tips. Place the wings in a slow cooker.
2. In a small bowl, combine the remaining ingredients. Pour over chicken and stir to coat. Cover and cook on low for 6 to 8 hours or until chicken is tender. Serve warm.

Sweet and Spicy Peanuts

Makes 1 L

Prep time: 10 minutes

Cook time: 1½ hours

INGREDIENTS:

30 g butter, melted
450 g salted peanuts
100 g sugar
55 g brown sugar
30 ml hot water
15 ml Sriracha Asian hot chilli sauce or hot pepper sauce
1 tsp. chilli powder

DIRECTIONS:

1. Place peanuts in a greased slow cooker. In a small bowl, combine the sugars, water, butter, hot sauce, and chilli powder. Pour over peanuts and stir to coat. Cover and cook on high for 1½ hours, stirring once.
2. Spread on waxed paper to cool. Serve warm.

Cinnamon Cheesecake

Prep time: 10 minutes

Cook time: 1½ to 2½ hours

INGREDIENTS:

8 digestive biscuits

60 g soured cream

2 large eggs

510 g cream cheese, softened

30 g unsalted butter, melted

150 g sugar, divided

½ tsp. ground cinnamon

Salt, to taste

1 tsp. vanilla extract

DIRECTIONS:

1. Pulse biscuits in a food processor to fine crumbs, about 20 pulses. Add melted butter, 15 g sugar, cinnamon, and pinch salt and pulse to combine, about 4 pulses. Sprinkle crumbs into a springform pan and press into an even layer using the bottom of a glass. Wipe out processor bowl.
2. Process cream cheese, vanilla, ¼ tsp. salt, and remaining sugar in the processor until combined, about 15 seconds, scraping down sides of bowl as needed. Add soured cream and eggs and process until just incorporated, about 15 seconds; do not over mix. Pour filling into prepared pan and smooth top.
3. Fill a slow cooker with 2½ cm water (about 500 ml) and place aluminium foil rack in bottom. Set pan on prepared rack, cover, and cook until cheesecake registers 65ºC, 1½ to 2½ hours on high. Turn off slow cooker and let cheesecake sit, covered, for 1 hour.
4. Transfer cheesecake to a wire rack. Run a small knife around edge of cake and gently blot away condensation using kitchen towels. Let cheesecake cool in pan to room temperature, about 1 hour. Cover with cling film and refrigerate until well chilled, at least for 3 hours or up to 3 days.
5. About 30 minutes before serving, run a small knife around edge of cheesecake, then remove sides of pan. Invert cheesecake onto sheet of greaseproof paper, then turn cheesecake right side up onto a serving dish. Serve.

Barbecued Smokies

Prep time: 5 minutes

Cook time: 5 to 6 hours

INGREDIENTS:

450 g miniature smoked sausages

300 ml water

800 g barbecue sauce

45 ml Worcestershire sauce

½ tsp. pepper

DIRECTIONS:

1. In a slow cooker, combine all ingredients. Cover and cook on low for 5 to 6 hours or until heated through. Serve warm.

Glazed Meatballs with Strawberry Jam

Makes about 10½ dozen

Prep time: 10 minutes

Cook time: 4 to 5 hours

INGREDIENTS:

1.8 kg frozen fully cooked Italian meatballs

375 g seedless strawberry jam

235 ml grape juice

235 g ketchup

230 g tomato passata

DIRECTIONS:

1. In a small saucepan, combine the juice, jam, ketchup, and tomato sauce. Cook and stir over medium heat until jam is melted.
2. Place the meatballs in a slow cooker. Pour the sauce over the top and gently stir to coat. Cover and cook on low for 4 to 5 hours or until heated through. Serve warm.

Dried Apricots

Serve: 6

Prep time: 5 minutes

Cook time: 3 to 4 hours

INGREDIENTS:

340 g dried apricots

1 strip lemon or orange zest

DIRECTIONS:

1. Put the apricots and citrus zest in the slow cooker and add water to cover. Cover and cook on low until plump and tender, 3 to 4 hours.
2. Turn off the cooker, remove the lid, and let the apricots cool. Serve.

Vanilla Chocolate Cheesecake

Serve: 8

Prep time: 5 minutes
Cook time: 1½ to 2½ hours

INGREDIENTS:
30 g unsalted butter, melted
2 large eggs
8 chocolate sandwich biscuits
510 g cream cheese, softened
115 g semisweet chocolate, chopped
135 g sugar
60 g soured cream
¼ tsp. salt
15 g unsweetened cocoa powder
1 tsp. vanilla extract

DIRECTIONS:
1. Pulse biscuits in a food processor to fine crumbs, about 20 pulses. Add melted butter and pulse to combine, about 4 pulses. Sprinkle crumbs into a springform pan and press into an even layer using the bottom a glass. Wipe out processor bowl.
2. Microwave chocolate in a bowl at 50 percent power, stirring occasionally, until melted, 1 to 2 minutes. Let cool slightly. Process cream cheese, sugar, and salt in the processor until combined, about 15 seconds, scraping down sides of bowl as needed. Add cooled chocolate, soured cream, eggs, cocoa, and vanilla and process until just incorporated, about 15 seconds; do not over mix. Pour filling into prepared pan and smooth top.
3. Fill a slow cooker with 2½ cm water (about 500 ml) and place aluminium foil rack in bottom. Set pan on prepared rack, cover, and cook until cheesecake registers 65ºC, 1½ to 2½ hours on high. Turn off slow cooker and let cheesecake sit, covered, for 1 hour.
4. Transfer cheesecake to a wire rack. Run a small knife around edge of cake and gently blot away condensation using kitchen towels. Let cheesecake cool in pan to room temperature, about 1 hour. Cover with cling film and refrigerate until well chilled, at least for 3 hours or up to 3 days.
5. About 30 minutes before serving, run a small knife around edge of cheesecake, then remove sides of pan. Invert cheesecake onto sheet of greaseproof paper, then turn cheesecake right side up onto a serving dish. Serve.

Chocolate Scones

Makes 4 dozen

Prep time: 10 minutes
Cook time: 1½ hours

INGREDIENTS:
800 g sweetened condensed milk
350 g milk chocolate chips
300 g crushed digestive biscuits, divided
2 (28-g) squares unsweetened baking chocolate, shaved
145 g finely chopped walnuts

DIRECTIONS:
1. Place chocolate in a slow cooker.
2. Cover and cook on high for 1 hour, stirring every 15 minutes. Continue to cook on low, stirring every 15 minutes, or until chocolate is melted (about 30 minutes).
3. Stir milk into melted chocolate.
4. Add 250 g of biscuit crumbs, a little at a time, stirring after each addition.
5. Stir in nuts. Mixture should be thick but not stiff.
6. Stir in remaining biscuit crumbs to reach consistency of bread dough.
7. Drop by heaping teaspoonfuls onto lightly greased baking sheets. Keep remaining mixture warm by covering and turning the slow cooker to Warm.
8. Bake in oven at 165ºC for 7 to 9 minutes, or until tops of the scones begin to crack. Remove from oven and cool for 10 minutes before serving.

Fudgy Brownies

Prep time: 10 minutes

Cook time: 3 to 4 hours

INGREDIENTS:

70 g plain flour

115 g brown sugar

1 large egg plus 1 large yolk, room temperature

60 g unsweetened chocolate, chopped

75 g unsalted butter

45 g toasted and chopped walnuts (optional)

½ tsp. vanilla extract

½ tsp. baking powder

⅛ tsp. salt

DIRECTIONS:

1. Fill a slow cooker with 2½ cm water (about 500 ml) and place aluminium foil rack in bottom. Grease a springform pan and line with greaseproof paper.
2. Whisk flour, baking powder, and salt together in a bowl. In a large bowl, microwave chocolate and butter at 50 percent power, stirring occasionally, until melted, 1 to 2 minutes; let cool slightly. Whisk sugar, egg and yolk, and vanilla into cooled chocolate mixture until well combined. Stir in flour mixture until just incorporated.
3. Scrape batter into prepared pan, smooth top, and sprinkle with walnuts, if using. Set pan on prepared rack, cover, and cook until toothpick inserted into centre comes out with few moist crumbs attached, 3 to 4 hours on high.
4. Let brownies cool completely in pan on the wire rack, 1 to 2 hours. Cut into wedges and serve.

Simple Pizza Bites

Prep time: 10 minutes

Cook time: 1 hour

INGREDIENTS:

450 g beef mince

450 g bulk Italian sausage

450 g spreadable cheddar cheese

4 tsps. pizza seasoning

½ tsp. Worcestershire sauce

DIRECTIONS:

1. In a large non-stick frying pan, brown beef and sausage until crumbly. Drain and place in a slow cooker.
2. Add remaining ingredients to the slow cooker and stir to combine. Cover and cook on low for 1 hour. Serve warm.

Walnuts Fruity Cake

Prep time: 10 minutes

Cook time: 3 to 5 hours

INGREDIENTS:

1 (517-g) package yellow cake mix

1 or 2 tins apple, blueberry, or peach fruit filling

120 g butter, melted

45 g chopped walnuts

Rapeseed oil spray

DIRECTIONS:

1. Spray the insert of the slow cooker with rapeseed oil spray.
2. Place pie filling in a slow cooker.
3. In a mixing bowl, combine dry cake mix and butter. Spoon over filling.
4. Drop walnuts over top.
5. Cover and cook on low for 3 to 5 hours, or until a toothpick inserted into the centre of topping comes out clean. Serve warm.

APPENDIX 1 RECIPES INDEX

Printed in Great Britain
by Amazon

52072225R00044